high-vibe feng shui ✦

11 Steps to Achieving Your Best Life

ASHLEY CANTLEY

The mission of Storey Publishing is to serve our customers by
publishing practical information that encourages
personal independence in harmony with the environment.

Edited by Liz Bevilacqua
Art direction and book design by Michaela Jebb
Text production by Liseann Karandisecky
Indexed by Samantha Miller

Illustrations by © Marina Muun
Author photo by Ashley Cantley (back cover)

Storey books are available at special discounts when purchased in bulk for premiums and sales promotions as well as for fund-raising or educational use. Special editions or book excerpts can also be created to specification. For details, please call 800-827-8673, or send an email to sales@storey.com.

Storey Publishing
210 MASS MoCA Way
North Adams, MA 01247
storey.com

Printed in China through World Print
10 9 8 7 6 5 4 3 2 1

Library of Congress Cataloging-in-Publication Data

Names: Cantley, Ashley, author.
Title: High-vibe feng shui : 11 steps to achieving your best life / Ashley Cantley.
Description: North Adams, MA : Storey Publishing, 2021. | Includes index.
Identifiers: LCCN 2020028942 (print) | LCCN 2020028943 (ebook) | ISBN 9781635862386 (paperback) | ISBN 9781635862393 (ebook)
Subjects: LCSH: Feng shui. | Well-being—Miscellanea.
Classification: LCC BF1779.F4 C36 2021 (print) | LCC BF1779.F4 (ebook) | DDC 133.3/337—dc23
LC record available at https://lccn.loc.gov/2020028942
LC ebook record available at https://lccn.loc.gov/2020028943

Contents

Dedicated with Love

To my husband, Thomas, and my son, Snow, who remind me that "when love speaks, the voice of all the gods makes heaven drowsy with the harmony" (FROM *LOVE'S LABOUR'S LOST* BY WILLIAM SHAKESPEARE)

FOREWORD

I *love* this book.

I feel an instant connection to Ashley and the way she maps out a unique approach to the art of Feng Shui in a way that's modern and entirely high vibe. Like Ashley, I believe it is within your reach to live in flow with your life rather than feel like you're moving against the current. The key to achieving balance and unlocking abundance is tapping into your intuition, releasing all that weighs heavy on you, surrendering to your magic, and embracing the energy of your space. Ashley's modern lifestyle and design practice can fit in with your life no matter your background, design expertise, or style.

As a health and wellness expert, superfood entrepreneur, podcast co-host, yoga teacher, and mama to three beautiful children, my life is often busy and chaotic. My home is my sanctuary, and creating a space that has the ability to change my energy is what I'm all about. In my own home, I integrated the teachings of Feng Shui to evoke a feeling of openness and welcome. I focused on creating an experience in each room. But wow — there is something so unique that Ashley is able to do in this book. It's not your average home design and style book. She explores living in the flow of the universe as a customizable experience for anyone's desires and style, while embracing the elements of Feng Shui to access your most high-vibrational life.

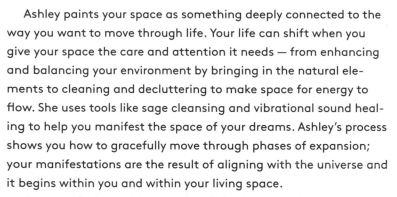

Ashley paints your space as something deeply connected to the way you want to move through life. Your life can shift when you give your space the care and attention it needs — from enhancing and balancing your environment by bringing in the natural elements to cleaning and decluttering to make space for energy to flow. She uses tools like sage cleansing and vibrational sound healing to help you manifest the space of your dreams. Ashley's process shows you how to gracefully move through phases of expansion; your manifestations are the result of aligning with the universe and it begins within you and within your living space.

As a certified practitioner, Ashley's fresh approach to Feng Shui embraces an intuitive process through guided exercises, helpful structures that are not rigid, and an energetically based map. Not to mention, this is a beautiful book to look at — the perfect addition to your coffee table.

Ashley believes that everything around you has the potential to affect your mood and energy. This high-vibe guide to Feng Shui will support you in clearing energy blocks within your space, living in your flow, and finding limitless abundance.

XOXO,

Sophie Jaffee, FOUNDER OF PHILOSOPHIE

Finding Your Flow

I wanted to write a Feng Shui book that was modern and easy to understand for the person who wants to transform their life using Feng Shui but who doesn't want a degree in Feng Shui (in other words, for the person who doesn't want to be bogged down with too much information). I wanted to write the book that I was look-ing for when I started on my journey but that didn't exist: a simple step-by-step guide to help readers learn how to shift the energy of their home in order to live a happy, balanced life that moves with the current, not against it. I wanted to create a guide to help you recover from heartbreak, find the love of your life, take your career to another level, to feel healthy, and live *in the flow*. Most of all, I wanted to write a book for those of you whom I cannot personally work with but who want to use the practice of Feng Shui to dra-matically change your life, as I did mine.

My goal is to teach you how to Feng Shui your space using your own style and give you all the tools you'll need so you can custom-ize your practice in the way that feels best for you. I believe this

book achieves all of this; if you follow the process, you're going to experience what it's like to live in the flow where all areas of your life feel abundant.

When I was in my 20s, my life felt lopsided. I had a successful career but was in a messy relationship; I looked good but was an anxious wreck; I lived near Central Park in New York City, but my apartment was deteriorating; I made money and yet I had none in my bank account. I was out of balance in every way, and it showed up in my mind, body, spirit, and space. I spent the entire decade of my 20s living like this, and, what's sad, in my circle this was the norm. I thought I had to make big sacrifices in order to achieve any kind of success in one area of my life, and when things got miserable I tolerated it, thinking "Only the strong survive." Thank goodness I figured out that life is meant to be abundant and balanced in all areas. When I found Feng Shui, I learned that creating clear intentions and directing my energy flow allowed things to fall into place. I'm now married to the love of my life, I have a baby, I'm creative, my career is soaring (on my terms), I have time to travel, I have a savings account, I'm healthy, and most of all I'm happy. When something does fall out of balance, I know how to bring it back into alignment. And — as if that wasn't enough — I know how to get what I want and manifest my goals with ease.

I've found my flow, and I'm excited to share everything I know about creating balance to help you find your flow and live an abundant life. Because I'm guessing if the universe led you to me, it's because you are craving balance; you want to feel like life is full and easy. The guide I've created for you is modern and yet based on an ancient system that I've simplified and pared down to offer you the essentials. You're going to change the flow of energy in your space to change your life. The best part is, there are no rigid rules, there is no traditional decor, you get to be creative, and you don't have to sacrifice your style. You're going to be able to change the energy of your mind, body, and spirit through your space. You can create a balanced home that will help you live a full life and manifest what you desire.

my path

I am a Certified Feng Shui Professional. I earned that credential through one of the longest-running Black Sect Tantric Buddhism (BTB) Feng Shui schools in the United States. BTB is a modern form of Feng Shui brought to the United States in the 1980s by Grandmaster Professor Lin Yun. I am recognized at the highest level, a Red Ribbon Professional, by the International Feng Shui Guild and am a member of the American Society of Dowsers.

I also have a career in network television, producing segments for *Martha Stewart Living*, the *Meredith Vieira Show*, and HGTV. I've worked with Showtime, Facebook, AOL/Huffington Post, MTV, and many others. And I've worked with top interior designers, including Drew Scott and Jonathan Scott of *Property Brothers*, Jonathan Adler, Thomas O'Brien, Jeff Lewis, and many more.

That's my résumé, but here's how I found Feng Shui: I became obsessed with holistic health, most likely because I was sick my entire childhood until I was diagnosed with celiac disease in high school. When I was 6 years old, I developed stomach pain that didn't go away until I was 16. During that time, I stopped growing, I became malnourished, my stomach was bloated, and my skin was ash gray.

This was before a gluten-free diet became mainstream and celiac was the number one misdiagnosed disease. I spent years visiting doctors who misdiagnosed me and prescribed everything from protein powder to eating more whole-wheat bread! The day before I went to the hospital in an ambulance, I closed my eyes and hoped I wouldn't wake up. Not in a morbid way, but in an I-need-relief way. When I was finally diagnosed at age 16, I weighed 59 pounds. Finding out I had celiac disease was the answer to my prayers. I finally started healing by adhering to a strict gluten-free diet. In the first three months of my new life, I gained 60 pounds by eating a pound of potatoes and a pound of bacon every evening for dinner.

By the time I reached my 20s I was vegan, eating a raw diet and drinking green juice. I practiced body brushing, used a tongue scraper, and started doing yoga. I lived in New York City, where I worked in the fast-paced, high-stress world of television booking and producing celebrities on TV shows, and I tried to soothe my stress with these holistic methods (sometimes successfully but mostly not). I studied Ayurveda, used crystals, had acupuncture, got deep tissue massage, and tried cupping. Then, at age 29, my longtime romantic relationship ended and I moved into my first solo apartment on the edge of Central Park near Lincoln Center. It was my dream apartment, and I filled it with happy mementos and painted the walls pink. I called it *my peace haven*. (New York City is yang energy, and my peace haven was the yin in my life; more on yin and yang later.)

On the heels of this newfound independence, I wound up entangled in a new relationship — too soon after my last breakup. That relationship lasted three years too long, the breakup was messy, and at the end of it my space was disgusting, my furniture ruined, and I had no idea who I was. My space was a literal mirror of my messy life. And that's when I turned to Feng Shui. I needed to rebuild my life, and I knew intuitively that I had to start with my apartment.

I bought a book and changed every inch of my apartment. I threw out old clothes that held toxic energy of dates past, bought new pink bedding, got rid of my furniture and plates, and started designing my space according to the principles of Feng Shui. With every new change I made, I also strengthened my vision of what I wanted out of life. And everything shifted.

After changing my space, within one year I had landed my dream job at the famed 30 Rockefeller Plaza and was making enough money to feel completely abundant. I traveled to Miami, Lake Como, and Turks and Caicos. I met the love of my life, got married, and got pregnant. It was everything I thought about as I was Feng Shui'ing my apartment. Something else happened: for the first time ever, I started listening to my intuition and to the signs the universe was sending. I moved out of New York City (I never thought I'd leave) to Atlanta and went deeper into Feng Shui.

Now my life is in balance and I've found the holistic lifestyle that I've been searching for. I have a family that I spend time with, I have a successful career, and I feel happy. I have a home that inspires me every day to share what I know about Feng Shui. Everything I've gone through has led me on this path to connect and share what I know with you.

Ashley

Feng Shui Works like Magic

Feng Shui seems like magic, but it's actually an ancient Chinese art and science that harmonizes the energy flow in your space. When you change the energy of your space, you behave differently. Studies show that depending on your environment, you're a different version of yourself. When I went to college in a small town outside of Pittsburgh, I was an underachieving version of myself. When I lived in New York, I was an overachieving career woman. Now, living in Atlanta in my Feng Shui'd home, I'm the balanced version of myself: motivated career woman, loving mom, devoted wife, and Zen (most of the time). It's the exact place I want to be. The beauty of Feng Shui is that when you consciously design your space with clear intentions, you can be whatever version of yourself you want to be. You can be an inspired world traveler, or a chilled-out vacay version of yourself, or a high-powered career woman. Your home triggers your habits and determines how you feel and how you act. So if you want to create a new habit, you can start by changing your environment. It's that simple: change your space and you will change your life.

So how exactly does Feng Shui work? You may have tried a few basic concepts, but it can be confusing with all the conflicting information out there. I'm here to simplify it: forget trying to learn difficult terminology or figure out which direction your bed should face. There are many different sects of Feng Shui, and I practice a modern version drawing from ancient Chinese methods, Indian methods, and shamanistic practices. Because Feng Shui is an art as much as a science, you can put your own spin on everything. You can forget Asian decor (unless that's your thing) or strict design rules. This guide is all about designing a space exactly the way you want it to look — and creating a space that you love where energy flows and new opportunities fall into your lap. You'll do this by paring down, using color, bringing in shapes, adding design elements, and, yes, even repositioning furniture. It can be as simple and budget friendly or as dramatic and luxurious as you want — the outcome will be the same.

three universal laws

Feng Shui works hand in hand with powerful Universal Laws. The **Law of Attraction** states that "like attracts like." In Feng Shui, this means that if you look around your space and see that it's cluttered, messy, or unharmonious, it's likely that you're going through something "messy" in your life as well. With this guide, you'll enhance areas of your home that correlate to areas of your life and you'll attract the "like" that you want. You'll enhance your space so that you start vibrating at the level you want to manifest in your life . . . which brings us to the **Law of Vibration**. Everything is composed of atoms, including your body. When you change your space, you change your level of vibration — you increase your personal energy and you become the vibrational match to the things you intend to manifest. When you change your space, you change your emotions (physical space has a profound effect on our emotions), and you start to feel really, really good. These positive emotions are charged up with positive vibrations that set you on a path to achieving your goals. But, most important, you must behave differently: the **Law of Action** states that in order to manifest what you want, you must take action! And here we come full circle. By practicing Feng Shui, you make intentional changes to your space that create and trigger new habits and you act differently in the world, you take inspired action, you make different decisions, you feel differently, you try different things, and — voilà! — you can manifest your dream life.

Did you know that 95 percent of the time, you are operating on a subconscious level? That means you are making conscious decisions only 5 percent of the time — or maybe even less! How many times have you driven in your car or ridden the subway or walked to work and have no memory of actually doing it? How many times have you realized you can't remember if you brushed your teeth, turned off the stove, locked the door, or fed your dogs? That's because you're moving through life letting your subconscious guide you. Feng Shui works on a subconscious level, affecting your subconscious mind. Your world is made up of energy, and when you intentionally shift your energy you can profoundly transform your life. In this book, we will work to change your space so that when you're operating on a subconscious level, your new space can speak to your subconscious and help old paradigms or habits drop away so that your life opens up in ways that you dreamed about.

common misconceptions

Feng Shui has existed for thousands of years, but there are a number of common misconceptions about the ancient practice.

Feng Shui Is Just Rearranging Furniture

The main goal of Feng Shui is to enhance your personal energy, and one way of doing that is by enhancing your space so that it has great energy flow. Yes, that means rearranging furniture, but it's also about bringing in the right design elements, using colors that you love that make you feel positive and balanced, and bringing in scents, shapes, and materials. Other ways of enhancing your energy are meditation, self-care practices, sage cleansing, visualization, mantras, mudras, nature, and blocking electromagnetic waves produced by technology. Feng Shui is a lifestyle practice, and you can dive into it as much or as little as you want.

It's Complicated and You Need a Compass

There are different schools of Feng Shui. While traditional schools use compasses and directions, I practice a modern version (BTB lineage) that blends principles from China, India, and shamanism. (A shaman connects the spiritual world with the physical world using ancient wisdom.) I teach you how to align the bagua, or as I call it, the Energy Map, based on how energy flows in your home. You won't need to position your bed a certain direction because in my practice, the energy of your home is unique and can't be determined by a direction. This approach is simple, tailored to you, and effective.

You Have to Decorate Using a Specific Style

The only style you need to Feng Shui your home is your own! You'll gain all the information and tools so that you can create an energetically flowing home (and life) using your own decor choices. Yes, there are traditional Feng Shui fixes like using Chinese bamboo flutes, dragon images, or other Asian-inspired decor to change the energy of a space, but I don't use them in my practice because I don't particularly like the style.

Feng Shui Is about Superstitions

Superstitions are the beliefs that something bad will happen if you do not do something. Feng Shui is not about superstitions, and if a practitioner tries to tell you it is . . . run! Feng Shui is all about creating great energy in your mind, body, spirit, and space. When you change your energy, you begin to make different choices at a subconscious level and invite new opportunities into your life.

If Your House Has Bad Feng Shui, You're Doomed

When I first started practicing Feng Shui, I thought I was doomed when I learned that certain things about my home weren't energetically ideal. But there's a fix for everything: there are ways to change energetic flaws in every home. There are maybe one or two deal-breakers for me when it comes to buying a house because of energetic reasons (I talk about them in Part 4), and it's for you to decide if certain energy blocks are something you could live with. Ultimately it comes down to how you feel about your home, if you love where you live, and/or if you can make changes so that you do love it.

my modern approach

Now that I've told you what Feng Shui is *not,* let's look at my
new and modern take on what Feng Shui *is.* My practice is holistic, encompassing the mind, body, soul, and space. It is rooted in
Traditional Chinese Medicine, Indian practices, and science; and
I modernized it by weaving in spirituality, Universal Laws, neuro-
linguistic programming, and allowing for the art of interpretation
in design and intuitive understanding of energy. And yet you don't
need a deep understanding of all these concepts to have success
with my practice.

Incorporating Tradition

Feng Shui is an arm of Traditional Chinese Medicine (TCM), which I
honor and stay true to by using many of TCM's principles, including
one of the core focuses of my practice, the Five Elements. We will
explore the Five Elements in depth. I ditched the traditional concepts of Feng Shui that don't work for me like using a compass to
determine energy and traditional design decor like bamboo flutes
in favor of creating a practice that anyone can customize to work
with your home, your personal design style, and your intuition. The
main goal of my practice is to offer you the *tools* of Feng Shui and
help you tap into your intuition so that you can redesign your life to
one that you love.

A Balanced Environment

I use Feng Shui to balance the energy of a person's environment.
I define "environment" as everything that surrounds you and
everything that you come in contact with. This includes your
space and also — maybe not so obviously — things like your words,
your thoughts, and other people's energy. Bringing balance to

your environment increases your personal energy so that you can become the best version of yourself.

Energetic Alignment for High-Vibe Living

This practice will help you create a high-vibration environment, so that you move into energetic alignment with the life you want. Everything in our world is made up of vibrating molecules, even the things that appear solid, like our bodies, trees, tables, and chairs. The things that you can't see, like words and emotions, are also made up of vibrating molecules. Things with high vibrations move faster and are lighter, while things with low vibrations move slower and are heavier. In the spiritual community, it is understood that in order for you to feel good and achieve higher consciousness, you must seek out things with higher vibrations. Remember, "things" doesn't mean simply material goods but also actions, thoughts, and words. This book walks you through the steps to achieve energetic alignment with the higher-vibration things you want in life. In other words, by following the "Go High Vibe" action steps in this book, you'll raise your energy so that you can become a vibrational match to your high-vibe goals.

Find Your Flow

I created this book to help you "find your flow." Finding your flow is when everything clicks, opportunities flow toward you, life feels easeful, and you feel happy and balanced. It's not a cure-all for your life, but it's about bringing awareness to what you open yourself to, what opportunities you are blocking, and what opportunities you are welcoming into your life.

embarking on
the journey

This book is designed to be a manual for you to turn to again and again. I hope you'll use it to transform your life, and when you achieve your goals, turn back to the book to help you do it all over again. In Part 1 you'll reset your mind and prepare your space with high-vibe actions, which are important to clear away old energy so you can create a good foundation and start fresh.

In Part 2 you'll get familiar with your Feng Shui Toolbox, including a list of my favorite fixes — ways to fix energy blocks in your home or ways to enhance your space to supercharge areas of your life — that I use repeatedly. I will also introduce you to the Five Elements. Earmark this section, because you'll refer to it often as you work on your space. These are the tools that will help you create transformations in your space and life.

In Part 3 you're going to start transforming your space. First, you'll learn about the most common energy blocks that you may be experiencing; then you'll balance and enhance your space, paying extra attention to your bedroom, kitchen, and front door. I'll also offer some examples of how you can use elements of Feng Shui paired with what you're experiencing in life and your emotions to design an outcome that you want in life.

In Part 4 I'll show you how to continue evolving with Feng Shui as well as how it relates to other areas of your life such as children, friends, your closet, your phone, and your car. I'll offer tips on how to hunt for an apartment or buy a new home, my personal Feng Shui deal-breakers, and some of the most transformative Feng Shui rituals. Finally, I'll share a few other spiritual practices that I love and that will raise your vibe.

I'm so honored to lead you on this journey and excited for you to experience major transformations that shift your energy and help you live in the flow.

PART ONE

Mind-Set & Home Preparation

Buckle up, because you're about to experience major life transformations! If you commit to doing the work, these steps will help you draw in wealth, love, career goals, and all-around abundance. You might be tempted to skip ahead, but don't. These early steps are vital to manifesting your dreams. Keeping an open mind and resisting the urge to say "I know this already" are essential. If you "know" everything already, chances are you wouldn't be here now. You may have heard of a concept before, but I may say it in a way that inspires you to have a different understanding of it. So push through even if something feels difficult to you because those are the things you need to do most. Take as much time as you need to get through the "Go High Vibe" exercises, but do not slow down just because you are avoiding doing something.

I have tailored this plan based on my training and a modern practice of Feng Shui. There are many different types of Feng Shui. Though all branches are valid, you don't want to mix and match. I've simplified everything here: you don't need a compass and you don't need to know astrology or do date calculations. You just need to follow all of the 11 steps and be open to achieving everything you want in your life. Let's get started!

Realize & Clear Limiting Beliefs

Without strong intentions your goals will never materialize. Your emotions also have to be in line with your intentions. Though you may say you want something, if your limiting beliefs are really telling you it's not possible, you'll never achieve it. So let's get to clearing out those yucky paradigms.

Your subconscious brain is programmed from the time you are in the womb until you are seven years old. Scary, right? During this time, you're a sponge soaking in everything, and that is how your perception of reality is formed. So every time your parents or the people who raised you reacted to a situation about money, relationships, or love (to name a few), you learned "truths" about the world. Sure, you learn other things as you get older, but 95 percent of the time you refer to how you were initially programmed. Here's an example: Let's say you're constantly struggling with money. Maybe you can't seem to hold on to money — you earn it, then lose it. Or maybe you hit a wall in your earning potential, and no matter what you do you never earn more. Now look at the first seven years of your life and think about what you learned about money from your parents. Maybe you were raised by a single mother who was struggling to make ends meet so you saw that living paycheck to paycheck was a normal experience. Or maybe your best friend had an in-ground pool growing up and when you asked your parents why you didn't have one, they said, "In-ground pools are for doctors." So now you believe that an in-ground pool is out of your reach unless you become a doctor. You might even notice that your current home reminds you of your childhood home because your subconscious was drawn to the old paradigm, pattern, or model.

Where you are in life may be a result of those limiting beliefs, and those thoughts are creating paradigms that need to be cleared out before you start manifesting your dream life with Feng Shui. When you make changes to your space with Feng Shui, you will have strong intentions in place. You will know exactly why you are making changes and what you want the outcome to be in your space and in your life.

Go High Vibe

Clear Limiting Beliefs

Let these questions inspire you to write down all the limiting beliefs that you learned in childhood and adulthood. Grab a pen and journal and pour every ounce of energy into this. It's tough but worth it.

Career and Money

+ Are you where you want to be in your career? Do you feel too old /too young/not qualified enough to get the career you want? Do you believe what you want is possible? Do you work too much? Do you have enough work? Do you have trouble figuring out what you want to do?

+ Do you feel like you are learning new things regularly? Does learning come easy to you? Do you have the schooling, certifications, or training that you want?

+ How do you feel about the recognition that you get in life? Do you wish more people would recognize you for your work or efforts?

+ How are you financially? Do you have enough money? Do you live paycheck to paycheck? Do you feel like you have a financial cap?

Health, Wellness, Joy, and Creativity

+ How is your health? Do you feel well? Do you feel fit? Are you happy with your body? Are you as active as you want to be?

+ How has your life journey been? Has life felt hard? Have things come to you easily?

- ✦ How do you feel spiritually?

- ✦ How do you feel about travel? Do you travel for fun? Do you travel as much as you like? Do you travel too much?

- ✦ How do you feel about your creativity? Are you inspired? Do you lack inspiration? Is creating hard for you?

Family and Friends

- ✦ How do you feel about the people who come into your life? Do they help you? Are they jealous of you? Do people just want something from you? Do you have strong relationships? Do the people in your life make you a better person?

- ✦ How is your family life? Are the relationships harmonious? Is there friction?

- ✦ What are your thoughts on having kids? Do you want kids? Do you feel like kids are a burden? Do you want more kids? How do you feel about pregnancy?

- ✦ How is your romantic relationship or marriage? Do you fight? Are you affectionate? Do you feel fulfilled? Are you on the same page?

Now look at your limiting beliefs and realize that these beliefs are NOT REAL! These are the beliefs of your parents that were handed down to you and stuck in your subconscious mind. Ho'oponopono is a beautiful Hawaiian practice for forgiveness, reconciliation, and healing that can help you clear away these beliefs. The Hawaiian word comes from *ho'o* (to make) and *pono* (right). It's a very simple practice that can help you forgive your parents or childhood caregivers, forgive yourself for holding on to these beliefs, and open your heart up to new beliefs and possibilities. This practice can help heal relationships you've had with your family, money, love, or other areas. By practicing ho'oponopono, you're taking responsibility for your life, pushing away the ego, clearing out old paradigms, and shifting into new alignment. Here's how it works:

Sit in a quiet space with your list in mind.

Repeat the following statements as many times as it takes until you wipe away the list from your mind. Whenever the limiting belief comes up in life, repeat these words:

"I love you."

"I'm sorry."

"Please forgive me."

"Thank you."

Here's an example of what these words could mean: I love you, my parents, who did their best. I'm sorry to myself for acting on these beliefs for so long. Please forgive me for having these limiting beliefs. And thank you to myself for clearing them away.

You can give these words the meanings that make sense to you.

2

Create Your Personal Activation Ritual

An activation ritual intensifies and magnifies the changes you make by harnessing all of your energy and sending it out to the universe. I suggest using this practice every time you make a change to your space. Feng Shui works without an activation ritual, but it is said to work 70 percent better with an activation ritual. You can create your Personal Activation Ritual with four components: intention, visualization, mudras, and mantras.

Intention is the reason you do the things you do. Without intention, you move aimlessly through the world and you take what life gives you whether you want it or not. There was a three-year period in my life when I lived without intention: I never sat down and thought about where I wanted to go in life in a grand or even day-to-day sense. You know what I ended up with? A relationship that wasn't right for me, health problems, a struggling career, and absolute anxiety. It's only when I started getting crystal clear about what I wanted, setting strong intentions, and pairing that with Feng Shui that things started to fall into place.

What you say, how you act, and how you behave should align with your intentions. In the words of Tony Robbins, "Where focus goes, energy flows." If you're constantly focusing on things you don't want, such as talking to friends about how you don't want to live paycheck to paycheck, then the universe will continue to deliver you a paycheck-to-paycheck lifestyle. You have to create powerful intentions and focus on those, not on the lack of them. When you create powerful intentions, you'll start to make different decisions that'll put you on the path and vibration (Universal Law of Vibration rears its beautiful head!) of the things that you do want. When you know what you want and declare it to the universe, your subconscious goes to work for you and begins to look for ways to materialize it in your life.

A few years ago, I wanted to take my son to Colorado for his birthday. (His name is Snow, after all, and we live in Atlanta!) Immediately after setting that intention, I started hearing stories about Colorado and seeing pictures of Colorado pop up in my social media. Has this ever happened to you? It's not a coincidence! It's your subconscious and the universe working together. I actually received an unexpected check in the mail that I put toward a vacation in the Colorado mountains. Some may consider this simply a stroke of luck, but I believe that the universe conspires to put us in alignment with our intentions.

Go High Vibe
Create Powerful Intentions

Get specific and know exactly what you want and why you want it. "Take a trip" is not specific enough. That could mean an hour away to your cousin's house — hey it's a trip, right? Here's a better example: a trip to Breckenridge, Colorado, with my family this December. Now the universe and your subconscious know what to bring to you. Next, ask yourself why you want the trip. Your *why* helps you intensify your focus and keeps you on track during the sometimes "annoying" waiting period. By the way, learn to love that waiting period! As you get better and better at manifesting, the waiting period will get shorter and shorter.

When stating your intentions, always be positive and always state your intentions as if they are happening or have already happened. If you say, "I want to go on vacation with my son," you are saying you lack what you want and that's what the universe hears (not to mention it's a vague request). You'll always be wanting. Instead, state your intentions in either the past tense or the present tense. Using the past tense tricks your subconscious into believing you've already achieved what you want. So if you say, "I'm so thankful I booked my trip to Breckenridge yesterday," your subconscious will believe that to be true and you'll take inspired actions to make that true. Or state your intention in the present tense: "I'm so grateful I'm spending a week in Breckenridge with my son this December." Also, gratitude is the quickest way to put you in a positive vibration. By starting your intention with "I'm so thankful" or "I'm so blessed" or "I'm so grateful," you're in a high-vibe state.

Now, let's look again at your list of limiting beliefs (page 21) and turn those beliefs into powerful intentions. Be specific, know why you're creating these intentions, and state them in present or past tense. Narrow down the list to two or three that feel really good to you. Repeat your intentions to yourself as many times as it takes to feel real, write them down, and post them somewhere you can see every day. You're on your way to changing old patterns or habits and manifesting what you want.

the power of visualization

Studies show that when you use vivid imagination, your brain cannot distinguish between what's real and what isn't. So if you feel, smell, see, and experience real emotions when you're visualizing, your subconscious believes that you've experienced it. When Olympic athletes visualize their performance, the muscles that are required to do the skills they're envisioning actually trigger when they do the routines in their mind's eye. Studies also show that "mental practice" can be as effective as physical practice and that you can develop new skills and strengthen old skills simply by visualization. When you visualize, your brain chemistry changes and your body records it as a memory.

When you use visualization, much like when you create strong intentions, your subconscious starts to look for ways to make your dreams a reality. You're prompting your brain to identify ways to get you to your goals faster. The Law of Attraction and the Law of Vibration kick into gear and you begin to operate on a wavelength of the things you desire. You start taking inspired action. Are you convinced now about why you need to visualize? I'm hearing you say "Yes!" So let's Go High Vibe and get practicing.

Go High Vibe
Visualize

Find a quiet space and set aside five minutes in your day (or as long as possible until you get the hang of it) to do this visualization practice. I recommend doing it before bed. Wayne Dyer, the best-selling author and leader in self-development and spiritual growth, says that you marinate with your subconscious mind for eight hours every night, and the last five minutes before bed are vital in reprogramming your subconscious. Instead of dwelling on the things that went wrong that day, use the five minutes before bed to program your brain with your intentions so that your subconscious can start working while you sleep. Try this:

1. Pick an intention to focus on. Say it out loud a few times.

2. Close your eyes and create the scenario. Put yourself in the scene and use all of your senses to experience it. Feel the experience with your emotions. Play around with being in the scene and seeing yourself in the scene.

3. Have faith that your intention will manifest. Close out your visualization by saying aloud "And it is done," or say "This or something better."

4. Let it go, have faith, and practice patience.

the power of mudras

I always felt completely awkward when at the end of a yoga class I was told to do a mudra, such as hands in a prayer position hugged to your heart. I had no idea why I was doing it or what the purpose was, but I halfheartedly went along with it figuring it was something that would enhance my spirituality or make me at least look super spiritual. As it turns out, a mudra is now one of my favorite tools to use in Feng Shui. It's a gesture that intentionally redirects and shifts your energy flow. People, including the ancient Egyptians, have used these powerful hand positions for centuries. A mudra connects various nerve endings with each other and triggers pressure points on the body to change the flow of energetic current within you.

Did you know that hands in prayer position is a mudra? You might be familiar with the mudra often practiced during meditation: thumb touching middle finger. The cool thing about mudras is there are hundreds you can choose from depending on what your goals are. Using a mudra with your intention and visualization is the best way to bring what you want toward you because you're using all of your energy to channel it. I have three favorite mudras that I use depending on my intention and my intuition. You can use these or choose another one that calls to you — you can't go wrong when you use a mudra that you love.

Thumb meets index and middle finger, with other two fingers folded to palm.

Thumb and pinky touching, other three fingers straight.

KUBERA MUDRA is one of the most powerful manifestation mudras. Use it when you want to supercharge your intention. I love to use it with my wealth goals, but you can use it in any area of your life.

BUDDHI MUDRA is the one to use when you want to express something clearly. It's a beautiful mudra to elevate yourself through powerful communication.

Hands cupped, thumbs touching, left hand on bottom.

DHYANA MUDRA is also referred to as the "open heart" mudra. This is the one I use most often! Something about this gesture feels so good to me. Images of the Buddha often depict his hands in this position, and it draws you into deep concentration, inner focus, and peace.

the power of mantras

Mantras are phrases that you say aloud or listen to repeatedly in order to affect your subconscious mind. It is said that a mantra can have a profound influence on the people around you, animals, and even your space. You may have a mantra that you repeat over and over to yourself without even realizing it — and it might be something negative such as "I hate my body" or "I'm broke" or "I have no time." This kind of mantra lowers your energy. It's time to flip those mantras upside down and find ones that work in your favor. Best-selling Japanese author Masaru Emoto conducted a study on the influence that words and sounds have on water crystals (if you haven't heard of it, look it up!) and found that water reacts differently when spoken to positively or negatively. Water crystal formations were much more beautiful when positive words and sounds were spoken! Because our bodies are 60 percent water, you can imagine what negative words and mantras can do to your personal energy. Positive mantras have even been used to heal sick animals and people. In Feng Shui, positive mantras can help you manifest your goals by connecting you to the energy of your space and to the universal flow of energy.

Sanskrit is called the "language of vibration," and Sanskrit mantras are beautiful soft sounds that, when spoken aloud, vibrate at a high level. I love Sanskrit mantras because they connect you energetically to what you want in life. Speaking them aloud helps to bring your energy into alignment with the vibrations of what you desire. When you set yourself on the vibrational level of what you desire, the universe conspires to deliver what you want to manifest. If using a Sanskrit mantra doesn't feel right to you, then you can pick a phrase that speaks to you. Even though vibrationally Sanskrit is ideal, using a mantra that doesn't feel good will work against your intentions. Instead, you can choose a favorite phrase from a book, a movie, a religious script, a song, or whatever else calls to you and moves you. Once you have chosen your favorite mantra, repeat it nine times — in Feng Shui, the number nine represents heavenly energy. Five and nine are auspicious numbers in Feng Shui. In general, odd numbers are considered to hold more energy and therefore are more activated.

Here are the three mantras I use regularly:

Om Mani Padme Hum

This is called the "Six True Syllables." This mantra is said to contain the core of all of Buddha's teachings. It is believed to call on the Gods of Compassion. Use this mantra to channel unconditional love and to gain clarity and understanding.

Gate Gate Paragate Parasamgate Bodhi Svaha

This is known as the "heart calming" mantra. It is found at the end of the ancient Buddhist text the Heart Sutra and compels you to see that you are separate from your ego. Use this to channel compassion.

Everything's Working Out Best-Case Scenario

This is not a Sanskrit mantra; it was given to me by my favorite Spiritual Intuitive. But it resonates with me and reminds me that the universe always has my back.

your personal activation ritual

Congratulations, you have a Personal Activation Ritual! Now arrange your hands in the mudra of your choice, get a crystal-clear intention in your mind, visualize that intention, and then repeat the mantra of your choice nine times. Seal the ritual by saying "And so it is done" and/or "This or something better" and have absolute faith that your desires are manifesting. Perform this ritual every time you make a change to your space — whether it's a physical change like cleaning or Feng Shui or when you are setting a new intention for your space.

34

Go High Vibe

Create a Vision Board

Now let's strengthen your Personal Activation Ritual by creating a vision board. I like to do this on my computer so that I can set my vision board as my screen saver on my phone, too. There are some computer programs out there for vision boarding, and there's also something to be said for taking the time to go through paper magazines or other items and putting your energy into physically cutting out pictures and hanging them on poster board. You can create your board whichever way you prefer.

1. Focus on five things you want to manifest in your life.

2. Find images that represent your desires.

3. Pin the images on a board.

4. Perform your Personal Activation Ritual with each image as you pin it.

5. Hang the vision board where you will see it every day.

3

Tap Into Your Intuition

Your intuition is a power that will always lead you in the right direction. Also known as your gut instinct, your inner voice, a hunch, a funny feeling, your sixth sense, or your Third Eye, your intuition is that inner knowing about what's right without being able to logically explain it. Whatever you want to call it, intuition is a superpower you can access to help create massive positive life changes.

Your intuition is readily available to you at all times as a guidepost in making life decisions. It even helps you tap into the Universal Mind, a concept that describes a realm where all information that ever was or ever will be exists. Science calls this concept "non-local consciousness"; it is the theory that information and ideas are not created by the brain, but rather they exist independently, and the brain can dip in and pull the information when needed.

To practice Feng Shui, you *must* listen to your intuition because you're focused on creating the life (and space) that *you* want, not what somebody else wants. Yes, I will offer guidelines (maybe even some rules), but everything is up for interpretation and person-alization. Take this information and go with it, but if something doesn't feel right, tweak it until it does. For example, if I suggest adding the color pink to your space and you hate the color pink, trust your intuition. Follow that feeling and adjust my suggestion until it feels right to you. Think about other colors in the pink/red family and find one that resonates with you — maybe you'll land on peach. As long as your intentions are in place and you're making conscious choices, the color peach will work just as well as pink.

intuition and life goals

Another way to bring the power of your intuition to Feng Shui is in thinking about your life and using your gut to know what's working for you, what's not working for you, and what new goals feel right to you. Most people don't set goals because they don't know what they want. You are using Feng Shui to enhance every area of your life, so now's the time to listen to your inner voice and ensure you get what you want.

But what if you have no idea what your intuition is telling you? When I started working on myself, I was not very tuned in to myself. It's been my experience that everyone has a gut feeling when something *isn't* right. The feeling that you should take one direction instead of another is there as well; it's just a matter of whether or not you're listening. Even if you continuously ignore your intuition, it doesn't go away — it just makes it harder to distinguish when your intuition is talking to you or if it's your brain talking. We have about 50,000 thoughts a day, so it does take some training to create space in your brain for your gut feelings to come through. Your inner voice passes information to your conscious brain; and as easy as it comes, it goes. It can be easy to ignore or suppress your intuition. All through my 20s and into my 30s, I didn't listen to my gut feelings. This led to jobs I hated, slow growth in all areas of my life, surrounding myself with the wrong friends, and a messy three-year relationship. I can even remember the moment when my intuition was telling me not to get into that relationship — I knew it wasn't right for me and yet I ignored the feeling. When I found Feng Shui, it helped me begin listening to my intuition, and now I rely on intuition to guide all of my important decisions.

Your intuition is a muscle that you have to build. If your muscles are weak, I'll help you become a bodybuilder! And if you're already an intuition rock star, you can continue homing in. Let's Go High Vibe to catapult you to the next level!

Go High Vibe
Listen to Your Inner Voice

In order to allow your inner voice to come through, you have to make space for it to speak, and then you have to listen to it. Simple daily practices like yoga, short meditations, or working with crystals can strengthen your intuition.

Get Grounded with Yoga Poses

Child's Pose is a yoga pose that taps into your Third Eye. Ancient wisdom says that stimulation of this energy point, located between your eyebrows, helps you tap into your higher consciousness or intuition. To do this pose, sit on your heels with knees together or separated, inhale and stretch your arms up, exhale and bend forward (continuing to keep your heels and hips touching) reaching with your arms, place your palms on the ground, and touch your Third Eye to the ground. Ground yourself with seven to nine breaths. You can do this simple pose throughout the day.

Inversions also activate your Third Eye. A simple inversion is the Standing Forward Fold. Simply stand tall, shift your weight into your toes, and exhale while bending forward from your hips (not your waist). Take seven to nine breaths. Do this pose throughout the day.

Experience the Sacred Pause

It takes practice (continual practice) to quiet your mind so that deeper thoughts can come to the surface. The sacred pause is what you experience between moments. It's the slight pause that happens naturally between breaths, it's the time after the sun sets when it's not quite night yet, and it's that stretch of days after summer's ended but it's not quite autumn. It's the pause in between happenings when you experience stillness — and that's where the magic happens, when you stop thinking, doing, and experience just being.

To consciously experience the sacred pause, get in a comfortable seated position, close your eyes, and focus on your breath. Notice the pause in between breaths. Hold the meditation for as long as you can, building up to 15 to 20 minutes a day.

Work with Crystal Energy

Crystals help open up your energy so you can access your intuition — and purple is the color that stimulates your Third Eye. I suggest working with lapis lazuli, amethyst, quartz, or any other purple crystals that call to you. Simply holding crystals in your hand, placing the stones on your Third Eye, or creating a dedicated spot in your home where you can see the crystals can all create shifts that help your intuition speak to you.

4

Clean & Declutter

43

Don't underestimate the power of a good cleaning and decluttering: it is one simple and transformative thing you can do to shift the energy of your home. Tossing out stuff makes space in your life for new opportunities and people to enter. It clears space for energy to move around and offers a sense of lifting a heavy blanket off of you. It's freeing. Not only that, clutter has a psychological impact on your stress levels, physical health, and cognition.

I't's time to take inventory of your space. You'll need to take a look around and get rid of anything you don't want, you don't love, or you haven't used in ages. This includes clothes, appliances, decorations, cosmetics, paperwork, magazines, furniture — everything and anything! It's especially important to get rid of stuff you've acquired from people you don't like (ex-boyfriends or ex-girlfriends, toxic friends, or others). When you let stuff from exes sit around, your space holds the energy of that relationship; if it was a bad relationship, that's the vibe of your space.

So clear out the junk. Go through your closets, look under your bed, and look in your kitchen cabinets. We store stuff in these sneaky places and think it doesn't affect us because we don't see it, but the hidden junk can actually have a huge effect on your subconscious and can lift you up or drag you down.

a deep clean

We've heard the saying "Cleanliness is next to godliness." Some say this came from Christian teachings, but I've also heard that it originated during a plague as a way to protect people. Either way, when I walk into a clean space it's a holy experience. And cleaning is one of the first things you must do in Feng Shui. Studies show that when your space is clean you sleep better, make better decisions, feel less stressed, and feel less anxious. Like clutter, dirt and grime can throw you off balance, weigh you down, and cause toxicity in the mind and body. Before you do anything, give your space a deep clean.

Choose your cleaning products carefully, as most brands are filled with toxic chemicals. A new study found that the long-term effects of inhaling cleaning products on a daily basis is the equivalent of smoking a pack of cigarettes a day. If you're cleaning your floors with harsh products, the chemicals can enter your bloodstream through the skin of your feet. This toxicity can deplete your energy levels and encourage sickness in your body. Feng Shui is all about increasing your personal energy, and exposing yourself to any kind of toxicity lowers your energy. Children are especially vulnerable to chemicals and can develop long-term health problems from exposure to them. There are many green products on the market that you can choose from. Make sure the products you buy were not tested on animals. Animal-tested products can hold negative energy from pain and suffering — and that's an energy you don't want to bring into your home or your energy field.

Homemade Essential Oil Cleaning Product Formulas

You can make your own cleaning products using essential oils. If you're going to use essential oils, be sure that the oil is 100 percent pure, with no added chemicals, and that it's sourced ethically. Some of these recipes call for a protective blend, which is an essential oil blend used for immune support. You can buy one or make your own by combining a few drops of eucalyptus, clove, rosemary, and cinnamon oils.

ALL-PURPOSE KITCHEN SPRAY: Add ¼ cup of white vinegar, 1¾ cups of water, 25 drops of wild orange oil, and 30 drops of an all-purpose protective blend to a 16-ounce spray bottle. To use: Spray and wipe.

FLOOR CLEANER: Add 1 cup of white vinegar, 1 tablespoon of natural dish soap, 20 drops of a protective blend, and 20 drops of lemon oil to a 1-gallon container. Fill the container with water.

SIMPLE SOFT SCRUB: Mix 1 cup of baking soda, ¼ cup of liquid castile soap, 10 drops of lemon oil, 10 drops of lime oil, and 10 drops of wild orange oil to form a paste. Add more castile soap if needed. To use: Scrub, then rinse the surface with water.

Go High Vibe
Clean Top to Bottom

It's time for you to go through every inch of your space and clean it. Use nontoxic products and work your way around every area of your space where you plan to implement Feng Shui. Pay special attention to windows, corners, and mirrors. (You'll learn more about mirrors in Step 8.)

5

Energy
Cleanse

Have you ever had people in your house whom
you didn't like and after they left you could
still feel their vibe? Or you had a huge argument with your partner, kid, or mom, and now
the energy of your space feels off? Or maybe
you've been sick in bed, and when you're finally
better you want to cultivate a healthy, happy
space? Using sage or sound can cleanse a space
and reset the vibe.

After you clear the clutter and deep clean, you are ready to cleanse the energy of your space. You can use the sage plant and sound to reset the energy of your space.

Sage cleansing is a spiritual tradition that originated more than 2,000 years ago. Originally a shamanistic practice and Native American practice, it is now also a modern one. You'll need a bundle of sage (also called a sage wand), an abalone shell, and a feather. You can find these online, in many health food stores, and in crystal shops. To cleanse with sage, light a bundle of sage and use a feather to push the smoke around your space to clear out the negative emotional energy. Hold the abalone shell under the sage to catch any sparks that may fly off while burning.

Make sure your intentions are strong and work the smoke through the room clockwise. Use your Personal Activation Ritual (from Step 2) for maximum affect. The smoke is said to change the ionic composition of the room, similar to that feeling you get after a good rainfall. Scientific studies have also shown that burning sage can clear up 94 percent of the bacteria in the air. Sage your space, your dog, yourself, and anything else when you want to reset the energy.

Another way to cleanse the energy of a space is by using sound to reset the vibration and break up stagnant energy. Sound has been used for thousands of years in religious ceremonies, meditation practices, and healing rituals. You can use a small bell, a Tibetan singing bowl, a favorite classical song, or even clapping. Simply introduce sound into a space anytime you want to break up stagnant energy.

Go High Vibe

Cleanse with Sage or Sound

Work your way around your space in a clockwise direction cleansing it with sage. Spread the smoke into every corner, bathroom, and closet. Use a feather to spread the smoke around, imagining that you're ridding your space of any negative energy and releasing positive energy with the smoke. Let the abalone shell catch any sparks, or use it to rest the sage on while you're spreading the smoke around. If you're sensitive to smoke, use sound.

PART TWO

Your Feng Shui Toolbox

You've done some mind-set training and prepared your space — now you can learn the essentials of Feng Shui. There are specific tools you need to start transforming your space and your life. We will start with the Energy Map and what areas of your life correlate with areas of your living space, and we'll also learn about the Five Elements and other tools you can use to change the energy of your space.

Then we will get familiar with the Five Elements so that when you really start working with them in Part 3, you're familiar with the concepts. I didn't know about the role of the Five Elements in Feng Shui until I started serious training. They are the basics of Traditional Chinese Medicine, and you'll use them to balance your space. They offer so much flexibility in designing a space that you will love.

I will also let you in on my go-to Feng Shui tools that I use to energy align a home. These are not all the tools that exist in Feng Shui, but they're some of my favorites. You can see which tools call out to you and keep them in mind for when you get to Part 3 and begin working on your space.

6

Align the Energy Map to Your Space

When I first started practicing Feng Shui, I had no idea how to use an Energy Map (traditionally called a bagua) and could never find a simple explanation for what it was or how it worked. I'd spend hours looking at my apartment, trying to figure out where my love area was located. Lucky for you, I'm going to give you the information in the way that I wish I had it, in the simplest form.

You've probably seen an Energy Map before — it's a grid divided into nine squares, and each square correlates to an area of your life such as relationships, career, wealth, family, or fame. It was derived in ancient China using the binary code system. For simplicity's sake, I won't go into the science of it, but essentially, every part of the Energy Map ties directly to an area of your living space, and every area of your space correlates to an area in your life. Which specific sect of Feng Shui you study determines how you align the Energy Map to your space. My method is easy to understand, and with this Energy Map you can manipulate your space to fix or enhance areas of your life. This is where the fun starts!

the energy map

Each area of your space is tied to your life. Here's the general rundown of what each area means in life:

+ Family (middle left) represents your family, including your ancestors.

+ Wealth (back left) is tied to your finances.

+ Fame (back middle) is how people see you in the world.

+ Love (back right) is your romantic partnership.

+ Children and Creativity (middle right) is tied to your fertility, kids, and creativity.

+ Relationships and Travel (front right) is tied to all other people in your life as well as travel for pleasure or business.

back of house or room

front door

+ Career and Life Journey (front middle) is tied to your career success and the ease at which you experience your life.

+ Knowledge and Spirituality (front left) is how you grow as a person and how you connect with the spiritual realm.

+ Wellness (center) is connected to your well-being and is also tied to the health of all other aspects of your life, all of the eight other areas.

aligning the energy map

At the bottom of the Energy Map are Knowledge, Career, and Relationships. This part of the map is *always* aligned to the door or entryway of your space (figure A). You can shrink or stretch the map according to the space you are working with (figure B). I've offered a few examples to help you understand how to align the Energy Map in your space.

If you are working within a house, you will align the Energy Map to your entire first floor. You can also align the Energy Map in each specific room. If the layout of your house is entirely too complicated (maybe you have a rounded space or too many angles), focus on each room one at a time. If you align the map and there are missing areas of your space (figure C), don't worry! We will address how to fix this in Part 3. And if you have only one room you want to balance, that's okay, too (figure D). Generally, the first floor of a home is the most important space to balance, and then you can take it room by room upstairs.

Ways to Use the Energy Map

A

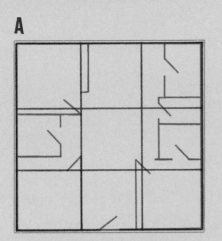

Align the bottom row of the Energy Map (Knowledge, Career, Relationships) with your front door.

B

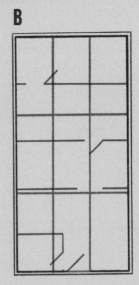

You can shrink or stretch the Energy Map to fit any kind of floor plan.

C

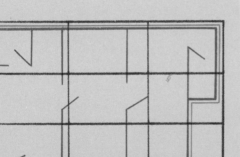

If your space has odd angles or a corner missing, don't worry. There are energy fixes for every circumstance.

D

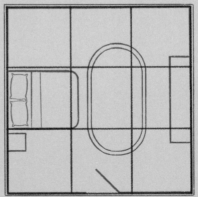

You can work with the Energy Map in a single room. Align the bottom row of the map with the entrance to the room.

Go High Vibe
Map Your Space and Set Intentions

Now that you know what an Energy Map is and how to align it, it's time to map your space. So let's get going! Draw the floor plan of your space. If you're working on a home, draw the entire downstairs. Don't get caught up on the details of the floor plan (like where each closet is), but do include every room and any notable angles. Next, use the Energy Map as a guide and draw it over your floor plan in another color. If you're not sure about which energy area a certain part of your space falls under, go with your gut feeling.

Set Intentions for Each Area

Once you've got your space mapped, it's time to set intentions for each area of your life. Think about each area of the Energy Map and what you want to manifest. Maybe there's a lot of fighting going on within your family and you want everyone to get along, or maybe you want to create a wealth corner with a specific financial goal, or maybe you want to encourage creativity. Grab a notebook and write down a specific desire for each area: Family, Wealth, Fame, Love, Children and Creativity, Relationships and Travel, Career and Life Journey, Knowledge and Spirituality, and Wellness. Hold on to these intentions; we will focus on them as you begin making changes to your space.

7

The Five Elements in Your Home

When I lived in New York City, I spent hours with my Chihuahua walking through Central Park. After an intense day of work I craved the grounding element of the earth. When I couldn't be outside, I brought the Five Elements of nature into my apartment by filling it with plants (wood), wrapping myself in a cozy flannel blanket (earth), meditating with candles (fire), taking long hot showers (water), and staring out my one big window at the sky (metal).

If you've ever read your horoscope, the concept of using Elements to describe energy and personality traits is not new. For example, the zodiac sign Taurus is an earth element sign; people born under this sign tend to be grounded, reliable, and practical. There are also water signs, air signs, and fire signs — I bet you probably know yours.

Feng Shui uses Elements to describe energy and personality traits, too. In Feng Shui, we use the Five Element Theory, which is the basis of Traditional Chinese Medicine (TCM). TCM is an ancient system that describes how energy moves within our bodies, our environment, our living spaces, and everything we interact with. Feng Shui is one of the eight limbs of TCM; the others are astrology, herbology, Tai Chi, meditation, diet, massage, and acupuncture. The Five Elements used in Feng Shui are wood, fire, earth, metal, and water, and we use them to understand the relationship between all things and to create a sense of balance (also called yin and yang). We also use the Five Elements to enhance areas of our lives or rein in aspects if we're feeling out of balance. We use the Elements of nature because they are, in themselves, perfectly balanced and they connect us back to our essence.

When your life feels out of balance, TCM teaches that it is often because an element in your mind, body, or space is out of balance, too. This imbalance can appear as anxiety, alcohol dependency, chocolate addiction, depression, stress, loneliness, anger, not feeling spiritually connected, feeling lonely, feeling fearful, feeling sick, lacking self-confidence, having fertility problems — the list goes on and on. The exciting thing about Feng Shui and the Five Elements is that they offer a specific and concrete way to get back into alignment with who you are and who you want to be.

Each of the Five Elements contains properties like colors, seasons, emotions, stages of growth and development, and sounds.

You can use these to balance and enhance your mind, body, spirit, and space. The various properties of each element allow you plenty of room to be creative in designing a space that balances your life, helps manifest your goals, and also suits your style. Before we learn how to use each element in Part 3, let's understand the basic properties. The properties related to the Five Elements are your guideposts, and you are free to play with them depending on how you interpret them and how they suit your style.

yin and yang

Every August as a kid I went to our local arts festival with my best friend to get our faces painted. We'd choose a simple image like the peace sign or the yin-yang symbol, which I thought looked super cool. Back then, I thought yin and yang meant "opposites." Years later, my best friend in New York referred to me as yin and her as yang: two halves of a whole that completed each other but also with overlap. Now I understand that yin and yang represent balance. In any situation, there is either yin energy, which is more passive like a still lake, or yang energy, which is super active like a crackling fire. You need both yin and yang energy to feel good in your life; otherwise, you feel off-kilter and issues like anxiety, exhaustion, boredom, or lethargy arise. For example, if you feel stressed out, you've probably got too much fiery yang energy and you need to add yin to your life for calming balance. Conversely, if you feel lethargic, you need to add yang to pep you up. The Five Elements represent different stages of yin and yang: new yang, full yang, yin-yang balance, new yin, and full yin. If you want to add just a little bit of energy to your space and life, you might turn to new yang. If you need a major burst of energy, add full yang. The same goes for new yin and full yin.

BASIC PROPERTIES

ELEMENT	ENERGY	LOCATION IN HOME	ENERGETIC LIFE CONNECTION	SEASON	HOW IT APPEARS IN LIFE
WOOD	new yang	• left middle • left back	• family • wealth	spring	• forest • trees • wood • tall buildings
FIRE	full yang	• back middle	• fame	summer	• fire • sun • candles • light
EARTH	yin-yang balance	• center • front left • back right	• health • wellness • knowledge • spirituality • love	early fall	• land • mountains • plains • plants • stones • crystals
METAL	new yin	• right middle • right front	• children • creativity • relationships • travel	fall	• earth metals (gold, silver) • anything made with metal
WATER	full yin	• front center	• career • life journey	winter	• oceans • lakes • waterfalls • creeks • swimming pools • plumbing

OF THE FIVE ELEMENTS

SCENTS	COLORS	SHAPES	MATERIAL AND FABRIC	ARTWORK AND IMAGES
• peppermint • jasmine	• green	• vertical columns	• plant-based materials	• trees • plants • flowers • tall buildings
• orange	• red	• pyramid	• faux animal print • faux leather	• fire • sun • desert • animals
• chamomile • lavender • patchouli	• blue • yellow	• square • rectangle	• granite • clay • ceramic • terra-cotta • velvet • flannel • tweed	• open land-scapes • mountains
• marjoram • bergamot	• white • gray • silver • gold • paste • tones	• circle	• metal • metallic • fabrics	• open sky • space
• juniper	• black • navy blue	• free-form • unstructured • flowing	• glass • mirrors • shells • coral • chiffon	• water-scapes • moon

Go High Vibe

Find the Elements in Your Space

It's time to get familiar with the Five Elements before you start using them to balance and create abundance.

LOOK OUT A WINDOW OF YOUR HOUSE. What Elements do you see? Outside my window I see trees (wood element), the sun (fire), the yard (earth), bird feeders (metal), and a creek (water). Make a list of what you see. Does one of these bring you some peace? Do you find yourself drawing on a particular element when you need something? For example, when I feel stressed, I go to the mountains. When I need perspective, I go to the ocean or a lake. And if I can't get out into nature, I'll sit with my plants or take a hot bath. Do you turn to one element depending on what you're going through?

NOW LOOK AT THE AREA OF YOUR HOME YOU PLAN TO FENG SHUI. It could be one room or your entire first floor. Using your Energy Map, walk through your space and write down which Elements you have in each area. For example, in my Career and Life Journey area (front center) I have yellow paint, which is the earth element; I have a wood table, which is the wood element; and I have a painting of a landscape, which is also the earth element. I realize that I have a lot of the earth element. Note where you see more of one element over another.

EVALUATE YOUR SPACE AS A WHOLE. It should feel balanced. You don't need an equal amount of every element, but notice if you have an overload of one element or none of another element. Do you have a balance of yin and yang? Look at your walls, pillows, artwork, and other decorations — are the colors balanced? Do you have a mix of wood, metal, and fabric? Don't overthink this; go with what feels right and balanced.

8

Create Your Feng Shui Toolbox

In addition to the Five Elements, there are many tools you can use to fix your space. You'll make good use of these to fix specific energy blocks. Don't be afraid to mix and match. You have the freedom to put your own style and spin on your Feng Shui practice and choose how you want to fix things.

When you have an energetic flaw or block in your space, when your space is off-balance, or when it doesn't feel good, you need to fix it. There are many ways to fix an energy block, and when you address a block you can also enhance areas of your life. If there's an area of your life that you want to amp up or a part of your life that is not as successful as you want, you can locate the corresponding area of your space on your Energy Map and fix it. For example, a few years ago the money flow in my life was basically nonexistent. When I looked at my space to see what could be blocking that aspect in my life, guess what I found? Every single one of my toilets was leaking and had poor water flow, and my sinks were clogging on a regular basis. The water element represents money in Feng Shui, and you want to make sure it's always flowing (more on this later). Those clogs were also clogging up my finances. Once I fixed my plumbing issues, lo and behold my finances did a 180-degree turn. When I addressed the negative energy in my home associated with wealth, the transformation of energy in my space cleared out blocks that I had on a subconscious and spiritual level about finances.

tools to fix energetic blocks and enhance your life

Water

Water holds a calming energy, also called yin energy, and yet it's extremely powerful. Think of the many powerful forms the water element takes in nature: waterfalls, lakes, and even streams that can carve into rock. Bring the water element into your space in the form of fish tanks, mini indoor fountains, or water walls, or channel it through images in artwork.

BEST USES

+ When you want to improve in the Career and Life Journey area of your home (see the Energy Map, page 56) or in areas where water is the Enhancing Element, which is the element that offers an energy boost. (We will delve into detail about how to work with Enhancing Elements in Part 3.)

+ When you want to call in wealth. In the principles of Feng Shui, the flow of water symbolizes wealth.

+ When you want to feel calm, peaceful, and relaxed.

TIPS

+ Because the water element corresponds to finances and money flow, make sure all the plumbing and water in your house are flowing well.

+ If you're working with images of water, make sure the water is flowing toward you and not away from you.

Plants

Plants and flowers hold so much good energy because they're alive, and they can be a great way to uplift the energy of your space. Plants are part of the wood element, and there are dozens of types of plants you can choose to use in your space.

BEST USES

+ When the energy of your space seems stale.

+ When there's an area of your life that is not thriving or needs enhancement.

+ When you have angled walls.

+ When you have odd-shaped rooms.

+ Around fireplaces to redirect the energy.

+ At your front door to bring more opportunities your way.

+ When you have a lot of metal surfaces or white surfaces: plants warm up and balance these spaces.

+ When you need to combat anxiety and feel calm and grounded.

TIPS

+ Avoid cacti or other plants that are sharp or have thorns; that energy creates conflict. If you're someone who absolutely must have cacti, place them in the Fame area of your space.

+ Do not use fake plants unless they look so real that people walk up to touch them to see if they're real. In my experience fake plants never look great, so I'd skip them if I were you.

+ Don't use dried plants or flowers because they're dead and you don't want dead energy in your home.

Light

When a home or space is dark and dim, it gives off a depressing or sullen energy and can create apathy. An area of your home that is dark and depressing will affect the area of your life that it correlates to on the Energy Map. Lights are part of the fire element and come in many forms and shapes — desk lamps, standing lamps, and overhead lights are all options to fix your space. You can even get creative and try fairy lights, candles, and glow-in-the-dark stickers.

BEST USES

+ When your space is dark or dim; even if you don't always turn the lights on, having them in your space makes an impact energetically.

+ When there's an area of your life that is not thriving or needs enhancement.

TIPS

+ Make an eco-conscious choice and use energy-efficient light-bulbs; it will help the environment and save you money.

+ Use a full-spectrum sun lamp during winter or if you're prone to feeling sad, to improve your health and mood.

Animals

Animals are alive (duh!), so, like plants, they have a lot of great active (yang) energy and are perfect to use when you need to enhance an area of your life or enliven an area of your space. You can use actual pets, animal prints, animal hide carpets (faux, of course), images of animals, or anything that represents animals (a horseshoe, for example).

BEST USES

+ When there's an area of your life that needs to be amped up.

TIPS

+ Place your pet's bed or house in an area of your home where you want to enhance energy.

+ Stay away from real animal fur, skin, or decor. Typically, the energy of how the animal was killed is not what you want to bring into your home.

+ Use animals that you love, and stay away from images of animals that are scary to you.

Mirrors

Mirrors are virtually synonymous with Feng Shui because they're a favorite fix for many Feng Shui practitioners. There are so many ways to use mirrors, and the bigger the mirror, the better. Full-length mirrors offer you the most power. Square, rectangular, and circular are the ideal shapes.

+ To brighten any area of your home.

+ To see what's behind you and who is coming or going in your space; for example, when you're sitting on your couch, working at an office desk, or cooking at your stove.

+ Above a fireplace to draw energy up.

+ To make an area of your home feel bigger; an expanded area of your home means an expanded life area.

+ To change the flow of energy: energy bounces off a mirror and goes elsewhere.

+ When you have a missing area of your home (see page 98 for this fix).

77

TIPS

+ Don't use a mirror that distorts images.

+ Don't use mirrors that have scratches, paint, or anything else on the surface (like art or designs over the glass).

+ Always check the reflection in the mirror. For instance, if you hang a mirror at your front door and the mirror is reflecting outside your house, all of the energy that's entering your home will bounce off the mirror and flow right back out the door. Adjust the mirror so you can't see the door.

Artwork

Artwork, including paintings and photographs, is an awesome way to change the vibration of your space. It's one of my favorite tools because you can get creative by incorporating other fixes or even the Five Elements into artwork to fix a space — and still complement your personal design style. You can use any style of artwork you like to bring your space into balance or to add oomph.

BEST USES

+ To add color.

+ To add any properties of the Five Elements to your space. For example, you could use abstract art that has pyramid shapes, which represent the fire element. Or you could use a photograph of a city skyline with tall buildings to invoke the wood element.

+ When you don't want to bring the actual element, such as animals or plants, into your space.

+ As a way to convey an emotion or feeling, such as love or inspiration.

TIP

Pay careful attention to the image in the artwork and make sure it's not conveying a message you don't want, including despair, anxiety, or loneliness.

Earth Crystals

Earth crystals are crystals we find in the earth (as opposed to cut-glass crystals, which are manufactured) and are one of my favorite tools because there are so many crystals to choose from, which means you can pick the one that calls to you or find the perfect crystal for your issue. Crystals strengthen your intentions. They have grounding energy from the earth element. Quartz, for example, emits a constant energy wave that can be detected with an electrical current. Some people claim they can feel the energy current when they're around certain crystals. For those who doubt that crystals have actual power, take a look at your digital devices: LCD screens are literally "liquid crystal display," and the electrical energy of the quartz crystal is used to keep time. So imagine how powerful crystals can be when used in your home. You can dive deep into the crystal world to learn about each stone's properties, or you can keep it basic and use the quartz crystal, which works well for a variety of fixes.

BEST USES

+ If your couch is up against a window, a quartz crystal placed on a shelf or floor behind the couch will prevent energy from going out the window.

+ If your bed is up against a window, place a quartz behind the bed on a shelf, windowsill, or the floor to prevent your energy from going out the window.

+ When you want to amplify any area of your life, find a crystal that correlates to that area of your life and use it in the appropriate area of your home (consult your Energy Map).

+ When you want to create a relaxing or serene space like in the bedroom or bath.

+ To ground a room if it's above a basement or garage, place a crystal in every corner.

+ To create an energetic level of protection or create security around your front door.

+ To inspire you in your office, to channel wealth, love, fertility, peace . . . the list goes on.

CHOOSING CRYSTALS

There are many crystals to learn about and work with. I recommend diving deeper and reading a crystal book, but here are a few of my favorites as a jumping-off point:

+ All-around energy elevating: quartz

+ To call in wealth: jade, citrine, green calcite, aventurine, tiger's eye

+ To call in love: rose quartz, chrysoprase, malachite, rhodochrosite

+ Calming: amethyst, blue lace agate, hematite

+ For protection: black tourmaline, shungite, selenite, bronzite, onyx

+ For fertility: moonstone

+ For grounding: smoky quartz, hematite, red jasper

TIPS

+ Find crystals online or at your local metaphysical shop.

+ Make sure the crystals you purchase are ethically sourced and the laborers are paid fair wages.

Cut-Glass Crystal

A favorite fix in my house is to hang a sphere of high-quality cut-glass crystal from the ceiling of a room in order to redirect, change, or enhance the energy of the space. Swarovski crystal, made in Austria, is what I use in my practice. It is a powerful crystal to use because of the superior quality of the glass. I use a sphere that is 1½ to 2 inches (40 to 50 mm) in diameter. Make sure to use real crystal; you'll know it's good if it throws rainbows around the room! If it throws out white light, it is likely made of plastic. This is one of the most powerful fixes because the faceted crystals redirect the energy of your space in many directions.

BEST USES

+ If the shape of your room is odd, you're missing corners, or something about the layout seems off, hang a crystal from the center of your room.

+ If you have slanted ceilings (especially in the bedroom) or wood beams overhead (both known to cause insomnia and health issues), hang the crystal from the ceiling or beam.

+ If you open your front door and there are stairs within a few feet in front of you, hang a crystal at the bottom of the stairs to redirect the energy.

+ If you want to enhance any area of your life, hang the crystal in the area you want to enhance.

+ If you open a door to your home and you see another door or window directly opposite that front door (most likely at the back of your house), hang a crystal in front of the back window or door to protect your energy from leaving.

+ If you have a lot of harsh angles jutting out from tables or any other furniture or decoration pointing at people, hang a crystal.

+ When you want to shake up the energy in your home.

+ When you want to feel happy! When the light hits the crystal, it shoots rainbows all over your home, which feels magical.

TIPS

+ If you buy cut-glass crystals online, good ones are usually certified, so you know what you're getting.

+ To add more oomph to your crystal, use a chain or a red string to hang it that's 7, 9, or 21 inches in length (remember, odd numbers are good in Feng Shui).

Chimes and Mobiles

Wind chimes and hanging mobiles are my favorite tool to shake up stale space. The movement and sound attract new energy as they sway in the wind. They can be calming or whimsical and fun depending on the style.

BEST USES

+ Energy becomes stale in long narrow hallways, so you can break up the energy with chimes or mobiles.

+ Sharp corners that jut into your space (like a table) create a cutting energy that can be diffused with chimes or mobiles.

+ To attract more energy in your life through your front door, because all opportunities enter through the front door of your space.

+ To deflect energy from flowing out your back door, hang a chime or mobile from the ceiling above the door.

Choose high-quality wind chimes, preferably brass; the sound they create will vibrate at a stronger frequency.

Colors

There have been many studies on how color affects our emotions and behavior, so it's no surprise we can use color to fix energetic issues. You're probably already using color fixes intuitively. Maybe you buy cheery yellow flowers to perk yourself up when you're feeling down; or maybe you use pink flowery wallpaper to lend a room a feeling of romance. Go with your gut — if a color makes you feel something that's missing in your life, use it.

83

+ **RED**: this powerhouse color vibrates at the highest level and holds a lot of energy. Red is great to stimulate any area of your life, to create passion, and for dark rooms (see more about red on page 84).

+ **GREEN**: growth, vitality, hope, new life, a fresh start

+ **YELLOW**: uplifting and cheerful or grounding and calming, depending on the shade

+ **BLUE**: serene, hopeful, knowledgeable

+ **PURPLE**: royalty, wealth, spiritual

+ **PINK**: the color of love, romance, marriage, and motherhood

+ **EARTH TONES**: grounding, calming, and serene natural earth colors

- **BLACK**: power, money, success. Black is a low-energy color, so if you are using a lot of it, be sure to balance it with other colors so you don't give off a depressing vibe.

- **WHITE**: purity, clean slate, openness, and new beginnings. This is another color to make sure you balance by using pops of other colors; otherwise, your space can feel sterile.

The Color Red

The color red, like the penetrating fire element that it's part of, is super active. It has a lot of energy — you could say it is very yang. Use red anytime you need more energy — or a variant like bright orange, magenta, or hot pink (whatever calls to you).

BEST USES

- When you want to feel stimulated, focused, and awake (like in an office).

- In any area of the home that's dark and needs oomph.

- In bathrooms to lift the energy from going down the drains.

- Use red strings to hang crystals from your ceiling to make the crystal fix more powerful.

- In the area of your home associated with fame (refer to your Energy Map to locate it).

TIPS

- Avoid using too much red in bedrooms because it will keep you awake at night.

- If you're prone to anxiety, avoid overusing the color.

Scent

Smell is a powerful way to change the energy of your space and your life. Think about how one waft of your grandmother's perfume could make you feel loved, or how the smell of clove can make you feel cozy. A bad-smelling space creates low energy, and a good-smelling space creates good energy (obvious, right?). Smell is one of the most powerful ways to trigger memory. If there's a smell that reminds you of something you want in your life, use it in your space. I have a candle in the Travel area of my house that I brought home from Paris, and I use it to channel another trip to that amazing city.

I also like to use essential oils because they're natural, as opposed to perfumes and some candles that are made with synthetic chemicals. Essential oils are highly concentrated (a small drop goes a long way), and I suggest using a diffuser. There are specific essential oils to create the perfect vibe for each of the nine areas of the Energy Map.

85

+ **WEALTH:** peppermint, wild orange, tangerine

+ **FAME:** orange, cedarwood, ginger, spearmint

+ **LOVE:** patchouli, rose, geranium, cinnamon, jasmine

+ **FAMILY:** thyme, clove, petitgrain, Douglas fir

+ **WELLNESS:** lavender, frankincense, myrrh, grapefruit, eucalyptus

+ **CHILDREN AND CREATIVITY:** bergamot, melissa, copaiba, clary sage, ylang-ylang

+ **KNOWLEDGE AND SPIRITUALITY:** chamomile, sandalwood, rosemary, dill

+ **CAREER AND LIFE JOURNEY:** juniper, lemon, coriander

+ **RELATIONSHIPS AND TRAVEL:** marjoram, cypress, lime

PART THREE

Change Your Space

I'm excited for you because now it's time to change your space! You've done the mind-set work, you have a list of goals you want to manifest in your life, you have an understanding of the Five Elements, you've got your space aligned to the Energy Map, and you have a powerful Feng Shui Toolbox. You're ready to identify the blocks in your home and fix them.

When you change your space, you'll feel the energetic effects immediately and new opportunities can start to show up in your life. Remember to have faith that your life is transforming and to acknowledge all the things that are coming your way. When you believe that what you want is coming, you will receive! Celebrate every single new opportunity that comes your way, whether it's more time with friends and family, new opportunities in your career, or acknowledgment from other people. Celebrating success brings more success because you are opening up your consciousness to receiving.

Let the fun begin!

9

Fix Common Energy Blocks

I can go into someone's home, see an energy block in their space, and accurately guess how it shows up in their life. When you have energy blocks in your space it can manifest in anxiety, sleep issues, moodiness, depression, relationship or health problems, career unhappiness, spiritual blockages, or many other ways. So it's important to address the blocks in your house first.

Blocks in your physical space stop energy from flowing. Blocks cause energy to get stuck in certain areas of your home, affecting not only your living space but also your life. Energy blocks show up in spots of your home that feel uncomfortable or give you a nagging feeling that something is off. Sometimes you don't realize you have blocks until you experience the relief of fixing them. Even if you aren't aware of them, these blocks can affect your subconscious and therefore your life in a negative way. Blocks also appear in your space as clutter or as design flaws and can wreak havoc on your life. Blocks in your space and blocks in your life are tied together — when you have a life block it shows up in your space and vice versa.

remember to use your intuition

In Step 3, you strengthened your intuition muscle. It's time to circle back to intuition because it's really one of your greatest tools when changing your space. There are a few ways you should rely on your intuition when it comes to changing the energy of your home.

First, when you start aligning the Energy Map to your floor plan, there will be times when you aren't sure which area of your space belongs to which area of the Energy Map. In this case, go with your gut feeling and make the decision. As long as the bottom of the Energy Map is at the front door, align it according to what feels right for your particular space.

Second, use your intuition to choose the Feng Shui fix that's right for your space. You might have a few different options to fix a flaw in your home, and for some reason one of those fixes is calling to you — go with that feeling. Or maybe you feel like you need to perform all of the fixes — go for it! Don't second-guess your gut feelings.

Finally, there will be times when you really don't like one of the fixes that I suggest. Rely on your intuition to tweak the fix to make it work in your home for your taste. Let's say you have a recessed front door and you hate wind chimes and pinwheels and the other fixes I offer. But you're at your local garden shop one day and you see something that you feel would attract energy to the front of your home and you absolutely love it — use it!

Using your intuition and having your intentions in place will always shift the energy of your home. So although there are guidelines to Feng Shui fixes, as long as a fix feels good to you and you know that your intention is to fix a block and you focus on what you want to manifest in your space and your life, it will absolutely work for you. Because if you hate a fix and use it in your space anyway, you'll bring negative energy into your space. Go with your intuition and make a fix work for you!

the blocks

There are a few common energy blocks to look out for, and because no home is perfect, your space probably has one or two of these issues that you'll need to fix. The blocks that I see the most are also the ones that have the biggest energetic impact in your space; fixing these can create dramatic change.

So now you're going to identify which blocks appear in your home, decide how to fix the block using your Feng Shui Toolbox, and make the fix. Remember to perform all these steps every time you fix an energetic block:

1.   Make sure your intentions are in place and know why you are fixing something.

2.   Fix the energetic block using your Feng Shui Toolbox.

3.   Seal the action with your Personal Activation Ritual.

4.   Have faith that the energy has changed, and that balance and opportunities are coming your way.

Your Back Is Facing the Door

It's important to be in a commanding position where you can see who is coming and going in your space while you're sitting. Sitting with your back to the door creates anxiety that seeps into your subconscious. It creates tension in your body and your mind because you always have to be on alert, or you get startled when someone walks up behind you.

THE FIX: Arrange every couch, chair, ottoman, bed, desk, and loveseat in the room so that you can see the door wherever you're sitting.

ALTERNATIVE FIX: Sometimes small spaces have limited options, so if you can't change the arrangement of your space, place a mirror in front of the furniture so that you can see behind you.

Staircase When You Open Your Front Door

If you open your front door and there are stairs within four feet in front of you, the energy from the top of the stairs will exit your home, taking good energy with it. This energy also moves fast, and when you open the door the energy hits you in the heart. Traditional Feng Shui practice says that this block can cause heart issues — whether or not you believe that, entering onto a stairway does feel jolting.

THE FIX: The goal is to redirect the energy coming down the stairs, and the easiest way to do this is to hang a cut-glass crystal from the ceiling at the bottom of the stairs. For extra oomph, you can use a red string in any length divisible by nine.

ALTERNATIVE FIX: Place an odd number (like one or three) of plants at the bottom of the stairway to break up the energy.

ALTERNATIVE FIX: Place quartz crystals at the bottom of the stairs to lift the energy up.

Beams Overhead

People love exposed beams, but if they're weight-bearing they can weigh heavy energetically on people sitting or sleeping below them. They're thought, traditionally, to cause health issues such as anxiety, headaches, tension, and arguments.

THE FIX: Paint the beams the same color as the ceiling so they blend in.

ALTERNATIVE FIX: Add standing lights to your space to energetically lift the beams up.

ALTERNATIVE FIX: Place clear quartz crystals under the beams to energetically lift the energy.

Plumbing Issues

Plumbing controls the flow of water in your home, which means the flow of money and opportunity in your life. Issues to look for include drains that clog, toilets that run (leaking money), leaky air conditioners, and any other problems with pipes, drains, and water flow.

THE FIX: Fix the issue.

Anything Broken

Broken things in your home lower the energy — that goes for squeaky doors, broken furniture, clothes with holes, dislodged cabinet doors . . . you get the idea.

THE FIX: Fix or replace all things broken.

Slanted Ceilings

Slanted ceilings can feel oppressive, like you have the weight of the world on your shoulders or as if the house is falling in on you. They can affect your mental health and cause insomnia (if they're in your bedroom) or anxiety, and it can feel like you have too much pressure on you.

THE FIX: Hang a cut-glass crystal sphere or a mobile from the slanted ceiling. I hung a purple dream catcher on a slanted ceiling in my house because it also happens to be in my wealth corner.

Blocked Windows and Doors

When you have blocked doors or windows, you are literally blocking people and opportunities from coming into your life. People often pile stuff near the door, block doors and windows with furniture, nail windows shut, allow windows to get dirty or grimy, or let shrubs and trees get overgrown in front of windows and doors.

THE FIX: Remove everything that's blocking windows or preventing doors from opening fully, both inside and outside your house. Doors need to be able to open 100 percent. Trim or remove any shrubs or trees that are blocking your windows. Clean windows and make sure they can open fully.

ALTERNATIVE FIX: A partially blocked window is not ideal, but if it is unavoidable, place a clear crystal quartz in front of the window.

Position of Doors and Windows

If you enter your front door and you see windows or doors of any kind directly in front of you, you want to fix these so that energy doesn't enter your front door and go right out the back door or windows. Keep in mind that all doors that open to your home, including garage doors, patio doors, and balcony doors, need to be fixed so that energy doesn't exit those.

THE FIX: To redirect the energy, hang or place a cut-glass crystal sphere at the door or window.

ALTERNATIVE FIX: Hang a wind chime at the door or window you can see from the front door to redirect the energy from flowing out.

ALTERNATIVE FIX: Create a visual block to the door or windows so you can't see them from the front door.

Hidden, Recessed, or Below-Street-Level Front Doors

The front door is where all opportunities enter your life. It's called the "mouth of chi" or "energy flow entrance." The front door should be easily visible, cheerful, and welcoming so you call the kind of energy you want into your home and your life. The best-case scenario is that you can see the door from the road, but often porches, trees, gates, or entrances below street level create blocks.

THE FIX: There are many ways to draw energy to your front door. Flags and pinwheels near your front door create movement that draws energy to your home. Wind chimes are a great option, as the movement and sound generate energy; I recommend using chimes made of brass, as they are super effective and resonant, but choose the one that calls to you. Adding color to your front door with flowers or paint attracts energy. Bird feeders and bird baths draw in energy from the heavens, which is super favorable. Trim all bushes so you can see the front door.

ALTERNATE FIX: If you live in an apartment building, you typically don't have much control over how your front door appears, so it's important that the entryway to your apartment be inviting. If you can, paint the door, add some sort of decor (not dried plants, though), add a happy doormat, and make sure it looks clean.

Bathrooms Connected to Bedrooms

Bathrooms connected to bedrooms are desirable, but plumbing can affect your energy in a negative way. You spend a lot of time in your bedroom, and if a bathroom is right there it can drain your energy.

THE FIX: Keep the bathroom door closed while you sleep. Close the lid on the toilet at all times. Avoid placing your bed against the bathroom wall.

ALTERNATIVE FIX: As you know, the color red is highly activated and draws energy to it. Red can be used in this fix on a transcendental level, meaning it can shift energy even when it's not readily visible. For instance, you can use a red permanent marker and draw a thin line around the top of the tub drain. This lifts energy up and keeps it from going down the drain. You want to keep all that great energy that comes in through the front door in your home.

Rooms above Garages or Empty Spaces

Rooms that are situated above garages tend to feel ungrounded because of the empty space below. You may live in an apartment where there's a parking garage or empty space used for utility purposes, or you might have a room in your home that's above a garage. All of these spaces need to be fixed.

THE FIX: Place a plant of your choice on the floor in every corner of the room to ground the space.

ALTERNATIVE FIX: Place a crystal in every corner of the room. Crystals with grounding properties include smoky quartz, shungite, jasper, and prasiolite.

Electromagnetic Fields

Electromagnetic fields (EMFs) radiate from common electronics such as phones, computers, and TVs, as well as from high-voltage power lines or radio/cell towers. EMFs can make you feel anxious, can make you lose sleep, and may even cause health problems. You can buy an EMF reader to detect high levels around your house, but you really don't need one to tell you where you keep your electronics plugged in. EMF energy needs to be fixed.

THE FIX: If you have a lot of electronics in your bedroom, it's best to remove them.

ALTERNATIVE FIX: Studies have shown that placing shungite stone near your phone or other electronics reduces your exposure to EMFs. Place a shungite stone in any area where a lot of EMFs are emitted in your home (like near the television).

Fireplaces

Fireplaces are like plumbing in that energy can leak out and all your hard work attracting great energy inside your home can escape.

THE FIX: Place a large mirror above your fireplace on the mantel to draw the energy upward.

ALTERNATIVE FIX: Place an odd number (like one or three) of plants at the base of your fireplace to redirect the energy.

Odd-Shaped Rooms or Missing Spaces

The ideal room shape is a square or rectangle, but you'll likely have a room in your home that is missing a corner or has some other irregular shape. When an area of your space is missing, the area of your life that the Energy Map corresponds to is also missing. For example, if you have a missing corner in your Love area, you may have relationship struggles. It's important to energetically fix these issues so the areas of your life can thrive.

THE FIX: Hang a cut-glass crystal in the corner of the room where there's a missing area. If you aren't sure where the missing corner is or if you have a slanted wall, you can hang the crystal in the center of the room instead.

ALTERNATIVE FIX: You can place an odd number (remember, odd numbers attract more energy) of plants along the wall where the missing area would be to attract more energy to that area.

ALTERNATIVE FIX: Place a large standing mirror against one of the walls where the missing corner is to fill in the area.

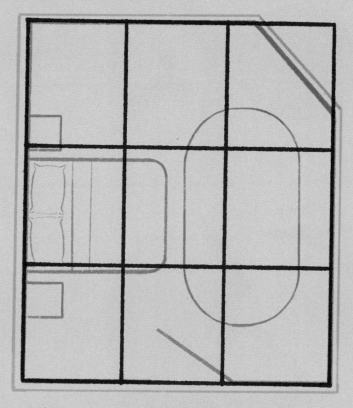

If a room is an irregular shape or has a missing corner, you can hang a crystal or place plants or a mirror in the space to redirect energy in a positive way.

10

Balance & Enhance Your Space

A balanced life is one where you don't feel like you need to make sacrifices in one area of your life to achieve what you want in another. I'm not saying you'll never spend a day working late or that you won't feel tired some days because you spent time tending to other people's needs like friends, family, or (in my case) a curious little toddler. I am saying that *as a whole* your life should look and feel balanced.

When I think back to my 20s, I see that I spent most of those years focused on my career and I ignored other aspects of my life. I stopped myself from exploring the world, taking vacations, tending to my relationships and romantic partner at the time, and building friendships. I gave up everything that made me feel great in the name of building a successful career. My mantras at the time — "I'm too busy" and "I can't afford to take a break" — gave me a false sense of superiority, and I felt noble for my sacrifices. I also truly believed that the only way to achieve what I wanted was to rise through the ranks while shedding my own blood, sweat, and tears. Now I know that true abundance happens when life is in balance, which puts you in the flow to allow opportunities to come to you effortlessly. Doesn't that sound much better than sacrifice?

signs of imbalance

Signs that you're out of alignment and need balance are exhaustion, anxiety, an inability to move forward in life, always wanting and yet never getting, an unfulfilled romantic life, friendships that feel toxic, and a general feeling of lack. Sometimes being out of balance is simply feeling bored in your life, feeling dissatisfied, and having an urge for more. You can change all these feelings by balancing your space to bring your energy into alignment so that you can attract what you want into your life.

balance your space using the toolbox

There are many ways to balance or amplify an area of your home to call opportunities into your life. You've got all the tools in the Feng Shui Toolbox, including lights, mirrors, crystals, and artwork. For example, if you want to enhance your spiritual life, you could consult your Toolbox and see that you can plug in a light to bring in energy and enhance the Spirituality area of your home.

balance your space using the five elements

You can also bring balance by using the Five Elements, which allows for more design customization and creativity. The Five Elements all have relationships to each other and specific ways in which they interact — they can nourish or deplete another element. A nourishing element means that it gives life to another element and thereby enhances it. We don't need to dive into the details of the relationships of the Elements here. (If you're interested, you can explore the relationships of the Five Elements in Feng Shui and TCM more in depth on your own.) For our purposes, it is important to know the Enhancing Element for each of the nine areas of your life and your Energy Map. This is the element that nourishes the element tied to the area of your home that you're working with. Using the example of enhancing your spiritual life, you can work with the earth element in the Knowledge and Spirituality area of your home and add earth's nourishing element, or as I call it the Enhancing Element, which is fire. You could bring in fire by adding candles, by displaying art images associated with the fire element, or by using the material, scent, colors, or shapes tied to the fire element. We will work through all nine areas of the Energy Map in this section to learn the Enhancing Element for each area and how to best bring balance to each area.

enhance your life by energetically enhancing your space

As you begin the process of actually working on your living space, there are two key principles to keep in mind:

1. Your home space is energetically linked to your life. If your life is out of balance, you need to begin by bringing balance to your living space.

2. Each area of your space is tied to one of the Five Elements, and every element has different properties associated with it, as well as an Enhancing Element.

As you work your way through each of the nine areas of the Energy Map in your home space, you have two main goals:

1. Make sure that the element associated with the area you're working is the dominant element present. For example, in the Family area, the dominant element is wood, so you want to be sure there is a good measure of that element present in the room.

2. In general, you want to create balance in every space. Ideally, each room should have a little bit of each element. Yes, a bit more weight should be placed on the dominant element, but too much or too little of any element throws your space and life off-balance. For example, you may want to use earth energy in a space that corresponds to an area of your life where you want to feel more steady and less anxious; however, too much of it can weigh you down and leave you unmotivated. Too little of the earth element can leave you feeling overwhelmed and scatterbrained.

There are many ways to incorporate the Elements into your space. You can bring in the actual element, or you can use images or artwork associated with the element, a material or fabric tied to the element, or scents, colors, and shapes. For example, let's say you have a reading nook and you want to bring balance to the space by incorporating all Five Elements. You could have a wood bookshelf to represent the element of wood, red pillows to call in the element of fire, a live houseplant to represent the earth element, a tall metal floor lamp to offer the metal element, and a blue armchair to represent the water element. This is your opportunity to get creative and use your intuition — if it feels right, go with it.

working with the energy map

Now pull out the Energy Map you created in Step 6 and look at the space in your home. The most effective approach is to work on the entire first floor of your house or your whole apartment, and align the Energy Map to your front entrance. I know not every living space is conducive to this method — and that's totally fine. If you have an oddly shaped floor plan and can't figure out how to align the Energy Map, then align it to the entrance of each individual room. Working room by room is just as effective, and you'll get the same results. You may even want to focus on only the one room where you spend most of your time. For example, if you have roommates and you want to Feng Shui your bedroom, or if you live in a dorm room, or if you have one room in your home that feels off and you want to fix it, or if you want to focus your efforts on one important space like the family room. There's no wrong way to do this — just go with your gut.

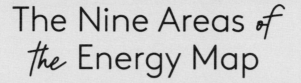

The Nine Areas *of*
the Energy Map

We're going to work through all nine areas of the Energy Map. Each area corresponds to a location in your home and an area of your life. Each area also has a dominant element and properties associated with the dominant element such as season, scent, colors, materials, and Enhancing Element.

Relationships & Travel

◼ LOCATION: front right side

This area of your home is energetically tied to all relationships in your life and to travel. Balance and enhance this space when:

✦ You have friendship troubles and you want to harmonize them
✦ You want to call in new friends
✦ You want more networking opportunities
✦ You want to strengthen your friendships
✦ You want to travel more
✦ You want to travel less
✦ You want to ensure safe travel

DOMINANT ELEMENT: metal

DOMINANT ENERGY: new yin

ENHANCING ELEMENT: earth

SEASON: fall

HOW IT APPEARS IN NATURE: earth metals (like gold or silver), anything made with metal

SCENT: marjoram

COLORS: white, gray, silver, gold, pastels

SHAPE: circle

MATERIALS/FABRICS: metal and metallic fabrics

ART: open sky, space

CHARACTERISTICS: The metal element is refined, simplistic, elevated, and beautiful. When out of balance, it can feel cold, rigid, and depressing.

ADD METAL TO THIS AREA: If you don't already have metal in this area, add it because it is the element associated with strengthening this area. Add more if you want to elevate your friendships, travel more, or cultivate simplicity in your relationships and the daily structure of your life (which could mean less travel if you're traveling too much).

DECREASE METAL IN THIS AREA: You already have a lot of metal element in this area and you struggle with relationships that feel surface level, cold, or restrictive. Your space feels cold or depressing.

KEEP IN MIND: Look at this space to see if you have any imagery that is counterintuitive to what you want in your life. For example, if you want to call relationships into your life, get rid of the painting of the solitary person and replace it with a painting of a social setting.

Other Ways to Enhance Energy:

+ Place pictures of yourself with your best friends in this area.
+ If you want to call more friends into your life, hang an image of a social gathering that you love. (I have a picture of Andy Warhol eating dinner with friends in New York City in this area of my home.)
+ Use photography or art that represents your favorite destinations or places you want to travel.
+ Put your travel purchases or mementos in this area.
+ Paint the room the color of your favorite hotel or destination to trigger the travel urge.
+ Decorate this space with the intention of creating social gatherings; you could put a beautiful vintage liquor buffet here (*Mad Men* style), introduce a record player, or arrange the chairs in a way that promotes fun conversation.

Career &
Life Journey

🔲 **LOCATION:** front middle

This area is tied to your career and your life journey.
Balance and enhance this space when:

✦ You want more career opportunities
✦ You feel confused about the direction your life is going and
  want more clarity
✦ You want a major life change
✦ You want your life to unfold with ease
✦ You feel sad about the direction your life has gone and you
  want to turn it around
✦ You love the direction your life is going and want to keep
  the flow coming
✦ You're having difficulty at your current job and want to feel
  more peaceful at work

DOMINANT ELEMENT: water

DOMINANT ENERGY: full yin

ENHANCING ELEMENT: metal

SEASON: winter

HOW IT APPEARS IN NATURE: oceans, lakes, waterfalls, creeks

SCENT: juniper

COLORS: black, navy blue

SHAPES: free-form, unstructured, flowing

MATERIALS/FABRICS: glass, mirrors, shells, coral, chiffon

ART: waterscapes, moon

CHARACTERISTICS: The water element is whimsical, meditative, and flowing. Out of balance, it's morose, shallow, or confused.

ADD WATER IN THIS AREA: When you want to call in clarity around your life and career and have it flow freely to you.

DECREASE WATER IN THIS AREA: When you feel overwhelmed with work, your life feels rocky, or you're feeling ungrounded.

KEEP IN MIND: Water is a powerful element in Feng Shui, and bringing in the actual element is an effective way to transform your life in this area. Many home stores sell mini decorative water fountains that plug into your wall; I recommend considering this as one option. You could also use a diffuser (this is what I do), a humidifier, a pet's water bowl — you can get creative.

Other Ways to Enhance Energy:

+ Take a look at the imagery in this area of your home to make sure it's conducive to what you want to manifest in your life. For example, I worked with a client who had a painting of a sailboat in rough waters about to capsize — imagine the kind of energy she's putting out in her life journey!
+ Hang artwork that is inspiring to your career.
+ Hang artwork that portrays the way you want your life to flow.
+ Set up your office, studio, or workshop in this area.
+ Keep your calendar in this space to plan your days, weeks, or months.

Knowledge & Spirituality

LOCATION: front left side

This area is tied to the wisdom you acquire throughout your life and your spiritual journey. Balance and enhance this space when:

✦ You're enrolled in college, taking classes, or learning something new and you want to succeed or understand it better
✦ You want to manifest the opportunity to enroll in a new class
✦ You want to bring in new understanding around something in your life
✦ You're looking for spiritual clarity or want to enhance your spiritual connection

DOMINANT ELEMENT: earth

DOMINANT ENERGY: yin and yang balance

ENHANCING ELEMENT: fire

SEASON: early fall

HOW IT APPEARS IN NATURE: land, mountains, plains, plants, stones, crystals

SCENT: chamomile

COLORS: blue, yellow

SHAPES: square, rectangle

MATERIALS/FABRICS: granite, clay, ceramic, terra-cotta, velvet, flannel, tweed

ART: open landscapes, mountains

CHARACTERISTICS: The earth element is grounding, peaceful, natural, and nourishing. Out of balance, there are no clear boundaries and energy feels stuck.

ADD EARTH IN THIS AREA: If your head feels like it's up in the clouds or your mind feels like it's spinning; if you need clarity or help sorting through your ideas; or if you want to create a grounding spiritual practice or want to feel more connected to yourself and your ideas.

DECREASE EARTH IN THIS AREA: If you feel stuck in your spiritual practice or your studies.

KEEP IN MIND: Make sure the images and artwork align with the vibe you want to create in your life in this area.

Other Ways to Enhance Energy:

+ This is a good place to keep books.
+ Create a reading nook here.
+ Set up crystals in this room.
+ Do yoga in this area of your home.
+ Place spiritual or religious items and imagery here.
+ This is a great spot for a children's play area or learning space.

Family

■ **LOCATION:** middle left side

**This area is tied to your family, including your ancestors.
Balance and enhance this space when:**

+ You want to create peace in your family
+ You want to create stronger bonds
+ You've had difficult relationships with members of your family, and you want to ease tension
+ You want to feel more support from family members
+ You want to honor your ancestors, keep their memory alive, and keep their energy with you

DOMINANT ELEMENT: wood

DOMINANT ENERGY: new yang

ENHANCING ELEMENT: water

SEASON: spring

HOW IT APPEARS IN NATURE: forest, trees, wood, tall buildings

SCENT: jasmine

COLOR: green

SHAPE: vertical columns

MATERIALS/FABRICS: plant-based materials

ART: trees, plants, flowers, tall buildings

CHARACTERISTICS: The wood element feels full of life, flexible, bold, spontaneous, and visionary. Out of balance, it can feel stagnant, constrained, or outdated.

ADD WOOD IN THIS AREA: If you're experiencing a major change within your family and want to help everyone roll with the punches; if you want to create inspired action as a family, like starting a new adventure together; if you want to shake things up; or if you want to strengthen familial relationships.

DECREASE WOOD IN THIS AREA: If your family members are feeling irritated with each other; if they're feeling stifled; or if they're stuck in certain behavior patterns and need to see each other from a different perspective.

KEEP IN MIND: This is the perfect area for the family to spend time together. If possible, create lots of room for people to convene here. Look at the imagery and make sure the energy is harmonious.

Other Ways to Enhance Energy:

+ Place family pictures in this area, including those of your ancestors.
+ Family heirlooms, family trees, or other items that connect you to your ancestry are perfect in this area.

Wealth

□ **LOCATION:** back left side

This area is tied to your wealth.
Balance and enhance this space when:

✦ You want to call in more money
✦ You want to create a bigger savings account
✦ You're having money struggles
✦ You have debt you want to pay off

DOMINANT ELEMENT: wood

DOMINANT ENERGY: new yang

ENHANCING ELEMENT: water

SEASON: spring

HOW IT APPEARS IN NATURE: forest, trees, wood, tall buildings

SCENT: peppermint

COLOR: green

SHAPE: vertical columns

MATERIALS/FABRICS: plant-based materials

ART: trees, plants, flowers, tall buildings

CHARACTERISTICS: The wood element feels full of life, flexible, bold, spontaneous, and visionary. When out of balance, it feels stagnant, constrained, or outdated.

ADD WOOD IN THIS AREA: If you want to be able to spend more money and still maintain a steady flow of wealth; if you want to create an influx of money; if you want to invest; or if you are making a big purchase.

DECREASE WOOD IN THIS AREA: If you feel like your wealth isn't growing or you are afraid to spend money.

KEEP IN MIND: Water is the Enhancing Element for wood and it's also tied to the energy of money. I highly recommend working with the Enhancing Element in this area.

Other Ways to Enhance Energy:

+ Look at the imagery in this area and make sure it aligns with what you want to call in.
+ Purple and green are great colors to use in this area.
+ Place anything that feels expensive and rich to you in this area.
+ Photographs or images that say luxury to you can be good here.
+ Put photos of yourself or your family in water here.
+ Citrine and jade crystals call in wealth and go well in this area.
+ Citrus is great here (it is a Chinese symbol of wealth); you can diffuse a citrus oil or place oranges or lemons (or images of them) in this area.
+ Amplify the area with lots of plants and lights.
+ Pilea plants, also called Chinese money plants, are perfect in this area.

Fame

LOCATION: back middle

This area is tied to fame, or how people see you and talk about you. Balance and enhance this space when:

+ You want more people to know who you are
+ You want to fix your reputation
+ You want to create a buzz around something you're doing
+ You want more attention

DOMINANT ELEMENT: fire

DOMINANT ENERGY: full yang

ENHANCING ELEMENT: wood

SEASON: summer

HOW IT APPEARS IN NATURE: fire, bright sun

SCENT: orange

COLOR: red

SHAPE: pyramid

MATERIAL/FABRIC: animal-based (use faux)

ART: fire, sun, desert, animals

CHARACTERISTICS: Fire is hypnotizing, attractive, warm, and stimulating; it's the center of attention. When out of balance, it can create anxiety, feel domineering, or be overstimulating.

ADD FIRE TO THIS AREA: If you want to draw more attention to your life; if you have a big project that you want recognition for; if you want to grow your social media following; if you want to attract more clients; or if you want to change the way people perceive you for the better.

DECREASE FIRE IN THIS AREA: If you're feeling stressed or anxious; if you feel burned out; or if you're being perceived as dominating or temperamental.

KEEP IN MIND: Red is a supercharged color and fits naturally in this area, so I recommend using it here.

Other Ways to Enhance Energy:

+ Images of people who inspire you work great here.
+ The fire element helps you bring your goals to fruition, so vision boards and visualization work are perfect for this area.

Love

◻ **LOCATION:** back right side

This area of your space is tied to your romantic relationships. Balance and enhance this space when:

✦ You want to get married
✦ You want to call in romance
✦ You want to strengthen romance or your marriage
✦ You've been arguing with your partner and want to create a closer connection

DOMINANT ELEMENT: earth

DOMINANT ENERGY: yin and yang balance

ENHANCING ELEMENT: fire

SEASON: early fall

HOW IT APPEARS IN NATURE: land, mountains, plains, plants, stones, crystals

SCENT: patchouli

COLORS: blue, yellow

SHAPES: square, rectangle

MATERIALS/FABRICS: granite, clay, ceramic, terra-cotta, velvet, flannel, tweed

ART: open landscapes, mountains

CHARACTERISTICS: The earth element is grounding, peaceful, natural, and nourishing. When out of balance, the energy feels stuck and life can feel out of your control in some areas.

ADD EARTH IN THIS AREA: If you want more love and energy to flow in your life; if you've been arguing with your partner and want to create harmony; if you need to create boundaries; or if you want to call in love.

DECREASE EARTH IN THIS AREA: If you feel like you're stuck in a rut in your relationship or your dating life; or if you feel like you can't find commonalities in your partnership.

KEEP IN MIND: Because pink is the color of romance, I suggest using it here; another color in the same family, such as peach or red, will work also. It is especially important to look at the images in this area and make sure they are sending out the energy you want to call in. For example, if you want to find love, images of couples work well. If you want to spice up your love life, an image of a tiger (or another animal that calls to you) could be fun.

Other Ways to Enhance Energy:

+ Wedding photos, or photos of you and your partner are perfect for this area.
+ Pairs of things work well (a pair of birds, two flowers).
+ Jasmine and rose are sensual scents that go well here.
+ Rose quartz crystals call in love.

Children & Creativity

▐ **LOCATION:** middle right side

This area is tied to children and creativity.
Balance and enhance this space when:

✦ You want to have kids
✦ You're having fertility issues
✦ You want to balance your child's temperament
✦ Your child is having behavioral issues
✦ You want to inspire your child
✦ Your children are arguing
✦ You want to feel inspired
✦ You're working on a creative project and you want it to go well

DOMINANT ELEMENT: metal

DOMINANT ENERGY: new yin

ENHANCING ELEMENT: earth

SEASON: fall

HOW IT APPEARS IN NATURE: earth metals (like gold and silver), anything made with metal

SCENT: bergamot

COLORS: white, gray, silver, gold, pastels

SHAPE: circle

MATERIALS/FABRICS: metal and metallic fabrics

ART: open sky, space

CHARACTERISTICS: The metal element is refined, simplistic, elevated, and beautiful. Out of balance, it can feel cold, rigid, and depressing.

ADD METAL IN THIS AREA: If you're working on a creative project and you want to take it to the next level; if your creative inspiration has run dry and you need to feel inspired; if you're trying to have a baby; if you have kids and they're arguing or have difficult relationships with each other; if you have a child who's lacking energy or needs uplifting; or if you want to increase your child's happiness.

DECREASE METAL IN THIS AREA: If you're feeling constrained creatively; if you feel uninspired; if you feel like you can't think outside the box creatively; or if your kids are depressed, moody, or are showing signs of perfectionism.

KEEP IN MIND: Make sure the images and artwork in this area of your home are conducive to what you want to call in.

Other Ways to Enhance Energy:

+ This is a great area to create new projects.
+ A children's bedroom or playroom would work well here.
+ Add images of children here to call in a pregnancy.
+ Place pictures of your kids here.
+ Add artwork or images that fuel your creativity.
+ Use calming scents here if you want to calm your children.

Wellness

■ **LOCATION:** center

**This area is tied to your health and wellness.
Balance and enhance this space when:**

✦ You want to increase your overall well-being
✦ You're recovering from an illness
✦ You want to create a strong foundation for all
other areas of your life

DOMINANT ELEMENT: earth

DOMINANT ENERGY: yin and yang balance

ENHANCING ELEMENT: fire

SEASON: early fall

HOW IT APPEARS IN NATURE: land, mountains, plains, plants,
stones, crystals

SCENT: lavender

COLORS: blue, yellow

SHAPES: square, rectangle

MATERIALS/FABRICS: granite, clay, ceramic, terra-cotta, velvet,
flannel, tweed

ART: open landscapes, mountains

CHARACTERISTICS: The earth element is grounding, peaceful, natural, and nourishing. When out of balance, there are no clear boundaries in your space (and life); one area runs into the next and energy feels stuck.

ADD EARTH IN THIS AREA: If you suffer from anxiety; if you want to connect to the energy of the earth to help you heal; if you want to ground, strengthen, or add peacefulness to every other area of your life; or if you want to connect with your core being.

DECREASE EARTH IN THIS AREA: If you feel stuck in your life; if you feel like you're not thriving; if you're gaining weight and don't want to or if you want to lose weight and you're having trouble; or if you feel weighed down emotionally.

KEEP IN MIND: Though this is the Wellness area, it's also the heart of your home or room and it affects all other areas of your life. You want to give this area a little extra care to make sure it's balanced so it doesn't throw off other areas of your life. Make sure you've tended to any blocks in this area. If the center of your home falls in a bathroom, I'd recommend lifting the energy and doing all plumbing fixes, including transcendental fixes (see page 93).

Other Ways to Enhance Energy:

+ Because this is such a vital area, I recommend hanging a cut-glass crystal sphere in the center of the room.
+ Use only uplifting images in this area.
+ Don't use dried flowers in this area.
+ Remove dying plants or flowers immediately.
+ Healthy plants are great here.
+ If you are manifesting your own personal health, display pictures of yourself at your best.

11

Home Hot Spots & Energy-Enhancing Tips

There are specific areas of your home that are especially important to tend — namely the bedroom, kitchen, and front door. There are a number of things you can do to enhance these hot spots to raise your energy and increase happiness in your life. A few other energy-enhancing tips will help you make the most of your Feng Shui practice.

Your bedroom (especially your bed), your kitchen (especially the stove), and your front door are three areas that have a big impact on your life that you need to pay extra attention to so that you can manifest your goals. Your bed affects your overall health — which makes sense because you spend so much time in it — and your marriage. Your stove is connected to your health and wealth because it generates a lot of fire and energy. And your front door is the "Entrance of Energy," where all opportunities enter your life.

Some other tips can amplify your practice, like fixing vintage furniture, giving your home a name, releasing emotions, and energetically separating one room from the rest of the space. Finally, I will show you how to approach Feng Shui by starting with an emotion or a real-life scenario that you want to change, and then working on your space to change the life issue.

the bedroom

Your bedroom should be a stress-free zone so that you can get restful, regenerative sleep to restore your health and feel revitalized every morning. It's also the place where you establish and strengthen your romantic partnership. One of the most important parts of arranging the layout of your bedroom is making sure your bed is in the correct position. Here are some basic bedroom tips, guidelines for your bed and placement of the bed in the room, and how to call in new love or strengthen existing love.

Bedroom Basics

+ Don't study or keep books in your bedroom; it's too stimulating.

+ Never do work in your bedroom; if you live in a studio apartment, create a separate space to work in.

+ Remove as many electronics as possible, including cords for digital devices.

+ Don't watch TV in the bedroom.

+ Create a sanctuary using calming scents. (I recommend lavender essential oil to relax and frankincense to regenerate.)

+ Place calming crystals like selenite and amethyst on your nightstand.

+ Be strategic with the colors you use depending on what you want in your life; consult your Feng Shui Toolbox when choosing a color for bedsheets or wall paint.

Your Bed

+ Wood bed frames are ideal.

+ Choose a strong, solid headboard because it signifies a solid foundation and affects your career, love life, and health.

+ A foot rail at the bottom of your bed should be avoided; if the foot of your bed frame extends above your feet, you can buy a pad to elevate your mattress, so your feet are above the foot rail.

+ Don't store things under your bed — this can create anxiety and poor rest — and don't choose a bed with drawers built under it.

+ Choose a bed that's not too high or too low, so that the energy can pass through easily.

Placement of the Bed

+ Place your bed in the commanding position so you can see who is coming and going from the room; if you can't put your bed in this position, place a mirror opposite the door so you can see from your bed who is coming and going.

+ Position the headboard along an interior wall so your feet are not facing the door; if this position is not an option, place something to visually block the door from the bed.

+ Don't place your headboard along a bathroom wall, because the plumbing and activity from the plumbing can drain your energy at night.

+ Don't place your bed along the wall that is the entrance to your bedroom, because the activity outside your bedroom can upset your sleep.

+ If space is limited and you must place your bed along one of these walls, hang a cut-glass crystal in the center of the room.

To Strengthen Love or Call in New Love

+ Add romance or passion to your bedroom with color, scent, and artwork; use pink or peach for love or fiery red for passion, scents including rose, and artwork such as flowers or animals.

+ Queen-size beds are best; king-size beds can create distance in a relationship.

+ Place rose quartz, the crystal of love, next to your bed.

+ Remove anything and everything associated with previous relationships from your bedroom; this includes items in your closet, under your bed, clothes, mementos, or gifts.

+ Create space for new love in your life by clearing an area in your closet, bathroom, or drawers for a potential partner's items.

+ If an ex-partner has slept in your current bed, get new sheets, a new bedspread, and even a new mattress if you can.

the kitchen

The kitchen is a central part of your home. It provides nourishment and fiery energy that fuels your health and your finances. When you prepare food for yourself or others, you are transferring your own energy into the food, so everything that happens in the kitchen (including your emotions) affects the food, which affects your overall health. If you're angry or stressed out or having a fight while cooking, imagine the kind of energy that gets transferred to your meal. Alternatively, if you feel loving, calm, and grateful while preparing a meal, that energy will flow. Here are some ideas to set up your kitchen for success.

Kitchen Basics

+ Keep your kitchen clean.

+ Choose calming colors to balance the fire energy of the stove appliances; active colors like red and orange can create anxiety.

- Consider where you shop for food because you take on the energy; I recommend buying produce at farmers' markets from people who have tended the crops with love. Buy organic if possible because pesticides lower your energy.

- If you shop at grocery stores, go to stores where you feel good and where the employees are happy.

- Eat cruelty-free; go vegan or vegetarian, or buy meat and dairy from ethical farmers.

Your Stove

- Ideally, your stove is in a commanding position so you can see who is coming and going; if you're cooking with your back to the door and you get startled, that anxious energy transfers to the food. If you can't see who is entering the kitchen, hang a mirror above the stove, use a mirrored backsplash, or put a small mirror on the countertop.

- Make sure the stove is functioning well and nothing is broken.

- Keep the oven, burners, and all elements of the stove clean.

- Fire up all of the burners regularly.

the front door

The front door of your home is where all opportunities enter in your life, so it's important to attract a lot of energy here. Even if you primarily use a back or side door, the front entry to your house still needs to be tended to. If you live in an apartment, do your best to make the entryway to your building and your apartment inviting.

Front Door Basics

+ Create a distinct walkway up to your door; slightly meandering paths are best because they create a gentle energy flow; long straight pathways are harsh and said to be "cutting like a knife."

+ Keep the area clean by sweeping regularly, and remove anything blocking the path to your door.

+ Cut back any plants that are overgrown or blocking the door.

+ If you have any front door energy blocks like recessed doors or below-street-level entrances, make sure to fix them (see the fixes on page 95).

+ Create a cheerful entryway with colorful door paint, a vibrant welcome mat, or flowering plants.

+ Attract energy to the area with a water fountain, a bird bath, a bird feeder, flags, or pinwheels.

Look at Your Front Door Inside Your Home

+ Make sure the first thing you see upon entering your home gives off the vibe you want; hang interesting artwork or use a paint color you love.

+ Make sure there's a closet or tidy space for shoes and coats.

+ Fix any blocks (see blocks and fixes on page 94).

energy-enhancing tips

These energy-enhancing Feng Shui tips and tried-and-true tricks of the trade can help raise your vibration when a certain area needs some extra attention.

Separate Energy between Spaces

Sometimes you want to separate the energy of one room from the energy of the larger living space. For example, if you live in an apartment and you don't want to take on the energy of other tenants in the building; if you have roommates and you want to disconnect your bedroom from the energy in the rest of the house; or if your garage is connected to your home and it's a total mess and you don't want that energy affecting you. I had a client whose mother-in-law lived in her house, and she wanted to create separation between her mother-in-law's space and the rest of the house. One fix to disconnect a room is to use a red Sharpie pen or permanent marker and draw a small circle on each side of the door frame mirroring each other, as if they are having a standoff. I used this fix when I lived in an apartment building, and I use it now to separate the garage from the rest of my home.

Fixing Vintage Furniture

My house is filled with vintage finds from my favorite stores in Atlanta and salvage shops in the surrounding country. Every piece of furniture holds a story, which can be good or bad depending on the previous owner's energy. Most of the time with vintage or secondhand furniture, you can't know what kind of energy you're getting. But there's a way to reset the energy. Put the furniture outside and give it a soap-and-water bath with a sponge and bucket. Then let it sit outside until the sun goes down. Then, sage cleanse the furniture and make sure the smoke gets all around and inside it. When you bring it inside, do the Personal Activation Ritual (see Step 2) and set an intention for the piece of furniture.

Release Emotions to Make Room for New

Holding on to emotion creates blocked energy that manifests in undesirable ways, including feeling stuck and not being able to move forward in life. I've had so many clients tell me that when they begin to Feng Shui their space, they also become super emotional. This makes sense because when you clear stuck energy from your space, you're also changing your personal energy. Let the emotions flow. Cry it out. Laugh it out. Write it out. Punch a pillow. Spend a few hours feeling whatever you need to feel. Shake out your limbs to help your emotions move through you and release the energy. Once you get rid of old stuck energy in your body, you'll have so much more room for new energy to flow.

Give Your Home a Name

I tell people that my home is like my best friend because she supported me in mending my broken heart, finding my husband, providing a sanctuary when the world felt chaotic, helping me to build wealth, and bringing me a lot of joy. When you start to see your home as an active participant in your life, you start to treat it with care and to make conscious choices about it. When you give your home a name, you bring it to life. Naming your home says that it plays an important role in your life. Your home becomes a character in your life with an energy force of its own (which you have control over). When my husband and I moved into our country cottage, we saw her as a quirky best friend here to make our family happy, and we named her Bernadette. I encourage you to name your home, too!

Minimalism and Collections

Personally, I'm a fan of minimalism because I hate having extra stuff in my home. I feel like it weighs me down and I want to feel mobile, like I can get up and go easily. I also prefer to be attached to experiences rather than to stuff. That's not to say I don't love beautiful things, but I carefully curate what I keep in my house. I know not everyone is or can be a minimalist, and that's completely okay as long as everything in your home has been consciously placed there. If you have collections and you love them, keep them. If you have collections that are unorganized and overwhelming your space, you need to go through everything and make sure you like it and get it organized in a way that makes sense for you. Feng Shui (and minimalism) doesn't mean you have to throw everything out; it just means you should love everything you have and that it all has an intentional place.

reverse engineering: start with your emotions or life scenario

Many people think that in Feng Shui you first have to start with your space in order to change your energy, but you can actually reverse engineer it and start with your life and your emotions, then go back to your space. Your space triggers your behavior, so you can design the life outcome you want by changing your space to trigger the feelings and behaviors you want.

Here are some examples of emotions or scenarios you may encounter and some fixes to your space to change what's happening in your life. There are multiple ways of approaching each scenario and many other options, but I'll offer some tips of where I would start. As always, go with your gut and start where it feels right for you — hopefully this will serve as a jumping-off point for you to begin to think about the approach of reverse engineering.

You're Angry with Someone in the Family

If you're feeling angry, go through your home and look at your plants. Do you have any plants with thorns, like roses or cacti? If so, remove them. Do you have a lot of clutter in your home? Look at the artwork in your home: Is it peaceful? If you're arguing with your partner, look specifically at your bedroom: Does it feel balanced? Does it feel too feminine or too masculine so that one person in the relationship doesn't feel seen or heard? Every area of the Energy Map correlates to a member of your family. Find the area and make sure it's clean, it's clutter-free, and everything feels balanced in the space. Have a look at these areas to address specific relationships:

Your romantic partner: Love

Mother of the household: Love

Father of the household: Relationships and Travel

Youngest daughter: Children and Creativity

Middle daughter: Fame

Oldest daughter: Wealth

Youngest son: Knowledge and Spirituality

Middle son: Career and Life Journey

Oldest son: Family

You Envy Someone in Your Life

If you envy someone, it means you want what they have. The good news is, when you feel envious, what you want is actually moving closer to you energetically — you're calling it near you. And you can do a little more work to call it in. Go through the mind-set work in Step 1 (page 19) to clear any limiting beliefs that are holding you back from believing you can't have what you want (if that's how you feel). Then look at your Fame area and make sure it feels good and that it's balanced, clean, and clutter-free. If you're friends with the person you envy, place a picture of you and that person in this area to energetically put you on the same vibration as that person so you can experience what you want. You can also go to your Career and Life Journey area and enhance the space to call in something different.

You're Anxious All the Time

If you're feeling anxious, go through your home and get rid of clut-ter or anything that's weighing you down. Then go through each area of your home to see if it's too yang — that is, vibrating with too much energy — and add some balance to it with yin. For example, do you have a lot of red, orange, or other colors in the red family in your home? Consider painting your space a more subdued color like an earth tone. Hang relaxing artwork like still water or land-scapes. Bring in soft textures to your space like cozy blankets and rugs. Add candles and diffuse a calming oil like lavender or anxiety-reducing frankincense. Bring in plants to ground your energy. Hang light-reducing blinds to block out any streetlights. Look at the center of your home: Is it well balanced, clean, and clutter-free? Is there something bothering you about your home? Get to the root of it. Maybe you're feeling unsafe and adding a home alarm system would ease your anxiety. Maybe hanging a religious symbol would ease your mind. Or maybe placing a tourmaline crystal at your front door for protection would ease your anxiety.

You Feel Bored with Life

If you're feeling bored, make sure the earth element is balanced — too much can make you feel stagnant. Call in and create new opportunities in your life by enhancing your front door and entry-way. Check that all doors and windows can open fully in your home, and wash the windows. Go to your Career and Life Journey area and add the Enhancing Element, which is metal. Change up the art in your space, the wall colors, the pillows, and any other furniture to inspire new thoughts. Meditate to break old patterns of thought and make room for new inspiring ideas in your life.

You're Confused in Life

Go through your home and make sure that the clutter is gone and that every area of your home is balanced and feels good. If you're confused about your career or next steps in life, enhance the Career and Life Journey area. If you're confused in love, fix any blocks and enhance the Love area as well. Stay open and see where your intuition leads you. Taking simple actions like changing your space usually triggers new ideas that shed light on where to go in your life. Immerse yourself in nature and seek clarity by doing one of the Rituals for Every Season in Part 4 (page 159).

You're Feeling Sluggish

If you're feeling heavy and sluggish, you might have too much earth element in your home that's weighing you down or making you feel stuck. Look around to see if this is the case. Particularly look at the Wellness area of your home and make sure it's clear of clutter. Add more yang to your life with vibrant colors, textures, and lighting. Design your space according to the way you want to look and feel. Remove any photos of yourself that are on display where you don't love how you look. Set up your space to trigger behaviors you want to encourage. You could set up a yoga or workout space or put your sneakers someplace visible and stock your fridge and pantry full of healthy whole foods.

You Want to Exercise More

The goal here is to create a space that triggers your subconscious to want to exercise, or to lift a barrier against doing it. If you like to exercise outside of your home — whether that's at the gym, the tennis court, or on a trail — find a place to keep your gear visible. Maybe it's near the door — you could hang your bike on the wall or keep your yoga bag on a hook or put your sneakers out, whatever it is you need. If you work out at home, find a space to create a permanent nook (or a whole room if you have it) and keep your yoga ball or weights there. If a room is set up and ready for exercise, it will trigger you to take action. If you have a gym or studio set up in your home and you're not working out, this means it has blended into your space and your subconscious isn't noticing it. Switch the location of your setup — even if you just move it from one corner to another. Use a stimulating essential oil like peppermint, or create a playlist of motivational music to help trigger you to get moving.

You Want to Heal from Sickness

When you want to create a sanctuary that restores your health, first and foremost you need to make sure nothing is broken in your home. If there are broken items, fix them. Fix any blocks in your home (see Step 9, page 89) or at least in the room that you spend the most time in. Clear clutter, clean, and cleanse your space to remove it of any sick energies that are lingering. Bring in colors of healing and vitality like blues, yellows, and greens with earth and wood elements. Bring life in with green plants and flowers. Diffuse relaxing and healing essential oils like lavender or frankincense. Open the blinds and let the healing vibes of the sun radiate and fill your space. If it's winter or your home doesn't get much natural light, get a sun lamp. If you don't have many windows, hang images of life in your space: birds, flowers, trees. Place images of you happy and healthy in your home. Align your mind-set with the outcome you want to create. Meditate and make sure that what you talk about and the words you use align with your health goals. Only surround yourself with people and things that raise your energy (see Feng Shui Your Friends on page 155).

You Want to Feel Happier

I love the idea of creating a happy home; this was the goal when I designed my own house. Use pops of vibrant colors and any colors that you love. Make sure everything you bring into your home makes you feel happy, and get rid of anything that doesn't. Donate or discard things that were given to you by people you don't like. Make sure all the images in your home are uplifting. Diffuse uplifting citrus essential oils. Create a space to show yourself some self-care, like a bathroom with your favorite lotions and crystals or a cozy reading nook filled with pillows. Add happiness to the front of your house with flowers, pinwheels, or flags, or by painting your door a great color.

You Want to Heal a Broken Heart

One of the major reasons I turned to Feng Shui was to heal my achy-breaky heart, and it worked wonders. Some people like to keep old memories of exes around, but I'm a firm believer that in order to move on you need to rid that person's energy from your space. If you're not ready to rid yourself of your ex's energy, then it may not be the right time to do the work in this section. Do some emotional healing, then come back to this when you're ready. For those of you who are ready, here's how to move on and call in your soul mate:

+ Get rid of every item your ex ever gave you.

+ Get rid of all clothing that reminds you of dates with your ex.

+ Get rid of all photos of you with your ex.

+ Delete your ex's phone number, texts, e-mails, and pictures from your phone.

+ Get rid of your ex's clothes that are still lingering in your space (yes, even that cozy shirt you sleep in).

+ Get new bedding, sheets, or bedspreads.

+ If possible, get a new mattress, or sage cleanse the old mattress.

+ Get rid of all furniture that your ex gravitated toward in your home, and if you can't do that, clean the furniture and sage cleanse it or transform it with a fresh coat of paint.

After you do all this, go to the Love area of your home and balance and enhance it to reflect the new relationship you're calling in. Then go to your bedroom and do the same. Keep your eyes and heart open for your new partner — they're on their way to you.

yay, you did it!

Congratulations on taking drastic steps to change your life. If you fixed all the blocks in your home, if you've balanced and enhanced it, and if you performed your Personal Activation Ritual, your home should already feel energetically different. Don't second-guess the choices you made or whether you did something right or wrong with Feng Shui — as long as your intentions were in place, you used your intuition, and you feel good about the changes, then you did it right. Keep your eyes (and mind) open now, because your life is about to change.

This practice has been life-changing for me. It helped me create a space that nursed my broken heart, launched me to my dream career, and brought in my soul mate. It has offered me a sanctuary to heal after childbirth and has brought pure joy to everyone in my family. I know that whatever you're going through, this practice can help you, too.

PART FOUR

Keep Evolving

Feng Shui is a living and breathing practice. It evolves with you as you continue to evolve as a person. You can turn to Feng Shui whenever you have a new goal in life, and you can realign your space accordingly. My home is constantly changing: I'm always swapping out artwork, rugs, pillows, or books to create the updated version of me that I want. Feng Shui can also add structure to your life and help you integrate various practices in a holistic way. It is a method of living that can expand into your food, your clothes, your phone, your car, your friends, and more. When I discovered Feng Shui, I realized that every area of my life is connected.

Beyond your home space, you can apply Feng Shui in other areas of your everyday life. And there are a few other spiritual practices you can use on a regular basis to enhance and change your energy. Finally, if you're apartment hunting or looking to buy a house, there are a few tips to keep in mind to guide you — and some of my personal Feng Shui deal-breakers when buying a home.

realign and reevaluate regularly

Have a look at your space every six months to one year and evaluate it. Think about each area of your Energy Map and the corresponding area of your life. How do you feel about it? Have you met your goals or have your goals changed? How do you feel energetically when you're in each area of your space? There are a few possibilities for your state of mind: You might be in the middle of feeling the changes that Feng Shui has triggered in your life; you may want to enhance your life even further; your goals may have changed completely since you last aligned your space and you need to realign your space; or your space could still feel off. If you're like me, you might constantly realign and reassess your home, and that's okay, too.

Experiencing Change

After you Feng Shui your space and you have faith that the intentions you set in place are coming to you, it's time for you to look for the changes in your life. Many people walk around with blinders on, never seeing the new opportunities flowing to them. Don't panic if there's a wait time before opportunities come your way. Trust me, your life *will* start flowing. Everything ebbs and flows, and a low will be followed by a high. Now that you've taken action, the ride will go up. Be sure to acknowledge the new opportunities when they do come your way, and be open to accepting more.

Further Enhancing Your Life

If you're already living in the flow, you might feel like it's time to create new goals and elevate your life further. Go to the area of your home corresponding to the area of your life you want to change and see if everything in the space reflects your leveling-up goals. For example, I made it to Colorado with my son for his birthday trip and crossed that goal off my list; now I dream of traveling with my father to Croatia to connect with our family roots. So I go to the Relationships and Travel area of my home, add inspiring photography of Croatia, and perhaps buy a Croatian record for my record player that sits in that area. If I had ever been to that part of the world, I would display photos of me from when I was there. Then I think about what other areas of my home I could enhance to help call in this trip. I go to the Family and Ancestor area of my home and set up photographs of my grandparents, who were from Croatia. I might go to my wealth corner and add another plant or a gold sculpture to call in a little more money to make this trip happen. Think about your goal, then think creatively about the different areas of your home you can tweak to align with your goal.

When Your Goals Change after You've Balanced Your Space

Sometimes, when you balance your space and bring the energy into alignment, it becomes apparent that what you thought you wanted was not actually meant for you. This can happen when there is something that's actually more aligned to your life, needs, and desires waiting for you in the wings. Facing the reality that what you thought you wanted is actually not going to happen can be difficult. I had a client who wanted to strengthen his struggling marriage, so he changed the energy of his space and it actually helped him become crystal clear that his relationship needed to end. Sometimes balancing and enhancing your space shines a light on how to move forward in your life in an unexpected way. When this happens, create new goals, then go back to your space and see what you can enhance or remove to call in the energy of what you want.

Work on Your Space Until It Feels Good

I worked on Feng Shui'ing my bedroom for months. I have slanted ceilings (which, by the way, is now a deal-breaker for the next home I buy), and I went through fix by fix to see what would work to make my space feel better. I was having trouble sleeping and felt like the ceiling was closing in on me; as a result, I was feeling immense pressure. I finally figured out what worked after trying every other fix: I painted my bedroom a dark shade of green. I painted the walls, ceiling, and baseboards all the same color to create the illusion that the slants weren't there, and that did the trick. But it took time to find something that worked, so keep going until things feel right.

148 apartment hunting or buying a home

No house has perfect Feng Shui unless you build it according to the principles of Feng Shui. So when you're house hunting, you can expect to see a few energy blocks that'll need to be fixed in any home. There's a fix for every Feng Shui block (see Step 9), but I actually have a few deal-breakers going forward. You should decide for yourself what energy blocks are deal-breakers for you.

Questions to Consider

Here are a few things to pay attention to when you're apartment hunting or looking to buy a home, before you even enter the house:

+ What's the vibe of the neighborhood? How do you feel when you enter the area? Go with your gut on this one.

+ If you're looking at an apartment or condo, how would you describe the energy of the building?

- Are there kids playing outside? Are your potential neighbors outside and do they look happy? How about pets? Do they look calm or on guard? Happy people and animals mean happy energy.

- Are the surrounding homes or buildings run-down?

- Are the trees, grass, and flowers thriving? If you're in a city, are there plantings around and a well-kept entrance?

- Does the neighborhood have any weird smells? (A neighborhood I lived in smelled like sewage at night, and some city blocks smell like garbage in the summer.) Bad smells are low vibe.

- Is there a cemetery nearby? Cemeteries have low energy, and people who live near them can feel depressed or be accident prone.

- Is the house near a church that has funeral services (also low energy)?

- Is the house near a school? Schools have a ton of energy and can create anxiety for those living nearby.

- Would you be near a fire department or police department? This could also create anxiety due to the nature of these places — responding to emergencies and dealing with a lot of frantic energy.

- Is there a backyard with a steep slope or drop-off? This can signify troubles holding on to wealth.

- Is there a clear pathway to the front door where fresh energy can enter? I've seen houses with no front door — not good.

- Is the garage separate or attached to the home? If the garage is attached, take note of its condition.

Here are a few questions to consider inside the home or apartment:

+ How do you feel upon immediately entering the front door?

+ Are there windows? What is the view?

+ Do you see any energy blocks? Are there a lot? Any that particularly bother you?

+ How does the energy flow through the space?

+ Does the space get natural light?

These are things to pay attention to that change the energy of your space. Decide what's a deal-breaker for you.

150 Deal-Breakers

When I buy my next home, there are a few Feng Shui deal-breakers that would stop me from considering living in a space. There are certain energetic issues that I don't want to deal with in my next home based on my experience: living next to a cemetery; slanted ceilings in the bedroom; and if the previous occupant experienced major hardship. Your experience and tolerance level might be different, and that's okay. You should go with how you feel.

I grew up within walking distance to the third-largest cemetery in the Unites States. It was beautiful, set in the rolling hills of Pennsylvania. I loved taking quiet walks there. I actually learned how to drive on the cemetery roads. Cemeteries can feel calming because they have very yin energy, or they can feel super depressing to some people. But I've known too many people who live near them who have experienced more accidents than usual in the form of broken toes, arms, and legs. I don't want that energy in close proximity to me.

Slanted ceilings in the bedroom are a never-again for me. My childhood bedroom had slanted ceilings, and I was drawn to a home with them. I thought of them as quaint and charming. But I've realized that they weigh me down, they cause sleep issues, they feel oppressive, and I have trouble breathing living under them. So never again.

In one place I lived, the previous renter experienced major health issues and hardships. I didn't know about this until after I'd moved in. I was constantly working to raise the energy in my space, and I never felt like I could get a leg up on the energy there.

Previous Owners' Energy

It is super important to consider the previous owner when buying a home. If you can, find out why they are leaving the apartment or selling the house, their experience in the house, and any other information related to their happiness. Owners who are selling their homes to move on to bigger and better opportunities, like a career move or expanding family, is good energy. Owners losing their home to foreclosure, getting evicted, getting divorced, or any other traumatic issue could mean negative energy. Also try to find out if anyone was gravely ill or died in the house of unnatural causes — that's negative energy, too. In my experience, when a previous owner suffered hardships, the current owner can suffer similar experiences unless they drastically shift the energy, which you can do. Hopefully, the home you want is not any of these low-vibe scenarios, but if it is — and I know a lot of people who buy homes that were in foreclosure — I recommend doing these fixes:

+ Clean and cleanse your home like your life depends on it. Make sure your intentions are in place when you sage your space and do your Personal Activation Ritual.

+ Consider calling a pro (like *moi*) to perform a specialized Feng Shui ritual like the Breakthrough Ritual (see page 166).

+ Enhance the areas of your home that the previous owner had difficulty with. For example, if the house was lost to foreclosure, enhance every wealth corner in every room. If the owners are selling because of a divorce, enhance every love corner in every room.

+ Create a spot in the Spirituality area where you can focus on protection and good energy for your family.

dress high vibe

One of my favorite ways to create the vibe and energy I want is through clothes, makeup, and nail polish. Look at your closet and make absolutely sure that you love everything in it. Weed out clothes that don't fit, clothes given to you by people you don't like (such as exes), clothes with holes or that are raggedy, and clothes that you associate with times in life that you didn't love. Only bring in new clothes that you love, and try to shop at eco-friendly spots. I actually arrange my closet by color so that I can choose a specific color depending on my mood or what I want to convey (refer to your Feng Shui Toolbox for color meanings). The same goes for nail polish. Red (the fire element) holds a lot of energy and represents the fruition of goals. When I'd wake up exhausted and had to go to an office or studio for work, I'd wear red, which lifted my energy and distracted people from noticing how tired I was. Black is my nail polish of choice when I want to get down to business. Yellow is for when I want to add sunshine to my day. The most high-vibe makeup and clothing is vegan, cruelty-free, and sustainably made.

carry a high-vibe phone or tablet

If you're someone who carries your phone or tablet around with you most of the day, you'll want to consider what kind of vibe it's giving you. The subconscious stress a phone can create is enough to throw your day off. First things first: if you have a smartphone, go through your contact list and clear out people you don't like — if they're good contacts, you can keep them on your e-mail list but not on the phone you're constantly holding. Then go through your messages and delete old messages — if you need to, take screenshots of important ones and save them as photos or e-mail them to yourself for your records. Messages are constant conversations that create clutter and take up space, and there's no need to keep them forever.

Make sure the image on your home screen and lock screen is one that you love or inspires you. Keep your apps organized and delete any apps that you haven't used in the last few months. Set the ringtone and all notification sounds to ones that you like and don't startle you. Remove any mean-spirited code names or ringtones (these may be funny jokes but are very low energy when it comes down to it). Remove e-mail accounts that you don't use on a daily basis. Set notifications only when absolutely necessary. Go through your photo files and delete any images you don't love, aren't high vibe, or that make you feel bad. Carry the crystal elite shungite with you to help block electromagnetic fields.

feng shui your food

In Feng Shui, the kitchen is one of the most important areas of your home because the energy in the kitchen can actually flow into your body through your food. Have a close look at your fridge and pantry for anything that is low vibe. If you use a lot of plastic, switch to glass containers and cloth bags. Pack your fridge with foods that are produced ethically. Fruits and vegetables are the highest-vibration foods to instantly raise your energy levels. Eat organic as much as possible. Produce grown organically has fewer pesticides, which lower your energy levels. If you can't eat all organic, try to stick with organic when consuming the "dirty dozen"; do a quick Internet search for the list of produce that is most susceptible to high levels of pesticides. Also, the less you cook your produce, the more nutrients you preserve. Traditional Chinese Medicine advises cooking and eating according to the seasons. Like nature, our bodies go through cyclical changes, so syncing with nature will help put your body in the flow. You can eat according to the Five Elements — as you know, every element is associated with a season and a color. Try to eat mindfully, rather than rushing through a meal. And try to create balance in each meal, using a little of each element to combine flavors and tastes.

+ In spring, channel the wood element and eat foods that are green and blue.

+ In summer, channel the fire element and eat foods that are red.

+ In late summer and early fall, channel the earth element and eat foods that are yellow.

+ In fall, channel the metal element and eat foods that are white (bananas, chestnuts, tofu).

+ In winter, channel the water element and eat foods that are dark.

drive a high-vibe car

I live in Atlanta, which means I spend a lot of time driving around in my car. When it gets messy — which happens often with a toddler — I notice I am more anxious and irritated with other drivers. Like your home, your car is a space that directly impacts your energy level and, in this case, your driving capabilities. To Feng Shui your car, clean the outside and inside with a nontoxic cleanser that won't weigh down your energy. Clean out any junk under the seats, in the glove compartment, and from any other pockets. If you have old parking tickets or citations tucked away, get rid of those. Throw away anything you don't need and organize your car like you would your home. Refer to the essential oil list (on page 85) to see what vibe you want to call in. I like calming scents in my car. Get an essential oil diffuser for the car or put a few drops of your favorite essential oil on a cotton ball and place it by the vent. Play music or listen to programs that enhance your vibe. If there are any service lights on, get your car checked out. Make sure you have emergency supplies in your car. Make sure your car payments are up to date. You might not think these things affect you, but your subconscious is constantly aware of them every time you get in your car.

feng shui your friends

Feng Shui is all about removing negative energy that weighs you down, and friends are no exception. Make a list of your friends and the people you surround yourself with on a daily basis. Ask yourself: Do you love them? Are you your best self around them? Do you feel rejuvenated when you're with them? Or do you feel like you've had the life sucked out of you after spending time with them? Use these questions to assess whether or not you need to gently remove people from your life. I know it can be tough, but if someone in your life isn't raising your energy, then they're depleting it and contributing to you not living your best life. In some cases, like with family members, you can't totally remove people. So create boundaries as to when you want to bring certain people into your life so that you can protect your energy levels.

I'm an open-minded person and a good listener, and that attracts a lot of people who want to unload their drama on me. Those relationships have not been reciprocal, so I've had to learn how to protect myself from attracting energy-sucking people. Every now and then, though, they still slip through the door. Sometimes they're family members or coworkers I can't totally avoid. If you experience the same thing, there are a few things you can do.

+ Visualize yourself in a protective bubble separating your energy from their energy. Selenite is a crystal that can help with this; carry it in your pocket or wear it as jewelry.

+ Create boundaries around how much time you spend with the person and what you will and won't talk about. You don't have to tell them this, but make sure you're clear on it before you see them.

+ Don't let them into your personal space if at all possible. If they must come into your home, use a black tourmaline crystal so that when you walk into your home your energy is cleansed, then sage yourself, and take a shower to wash the energy off.

raise a high-vibe kid

Children are very sensitive to the energy of your home, so it's especially important to create a space to help them grow, learn, and feel loved. When they're little, they're like sponges soaking everything into their own energy fields and subconscious brain. And when they're older, it's important to create a space that makes them feel in alignment with who they are.

Here are a few tips for young kids' bedrooms:

+ If you have a choice for which room to designate as a young kid's room, choose a room in the back of the house where it's a more protected area energetically.

+ Fix any blocks in the room, especially slanted ceilings.

+ Create a soothing space by using a lot of yin energy, including soothing colors, soft materials, and relaxing images.

+ Create a specific area of the room designated for play by bringing in the wood and earth elements to channel growth; wood channels learning and earth is grounding.

+ Keep the room as clean and clutter-free as possible; less clutter will help minimize emotional stress.

If you want to create a playroom for young kids, here are some tips:

+ Two great areas for a playroom are in the Children and Creativity area and the Knowledge and Spirituality area of the home.

+ Create balance in the playroom by using all Five Elements, but focus especially on bringing in the earth, wood, and metal elements.

- When your child is feeling overstimulated, remove electronics and bring grounding yin elements into the playroom such as nature finds, plants, and earth elements.

- If your child seems uninspired, bring in more yang elements such as wooden toys, vibrant artwork, and pops of color.

For older children, you want to make sure a room is in alignment with who they are at the moment. Here are some tips:

- If you have a choice of rooms, situate older kids toward the front of the house as they prepare to venture off on their own someday.

- Fix all blocks in their room and make sure it feels balanced.

- Get rid of old toys or things that are no longer developmentally in line with where they are now. Holding on to old things can inhibit their growth and keep them stagnant.

- Allow kids to express themselves by choosing the colors in their room, but help bring in balance as well. If they want a black bedroom, that's great because black is super relaxing, but too much of it can create lethargy or make a person feel morose. So help them choose vibrant artwork or pops of color to balance it out.

- Carve out a specific area in the room that's conducive to studying; the Knowledge and Spirituality corner of the room is a good place to do this.

Feng Shui is a lifestyle approach, and you can use it to help kids of all ages balance their energy. Here are a few recommendations:

- Diffuse uplifting, healing, or relaxing essential oils — depending on the need — in your family area, kids' rooms, or playrooms.

+ For younger kids, dress them energetically. For example, put them in calming yin colors or patterns at bedtime (I never put my kid to sleep wearing red). Or if they're headed out to play, dress them in vibrant colors that stimulate energy.

+ Plan nourishing meals to enhance their energy, and cook for them with love.

+ Introduce mindfulness practices like breathing and meditation at an early age. Transition times are a great time to do these, like after playtime and before snack time or before bed to relax.

+ Use sound and music to help harness their energy and relax their minds and bodies.

+ Do the Rituals for Every Season (below) with your kids. My son and I do these rituals together, and it completely calms his energy!

Integrating Feng Shui into kids' lives early on will help balance their energy, help them grow emotionally, and create a great foundation for them to build on the practice when they're older.

rituals for every season

I love connecting directly with the Five Elements to raise my energy level. Feng Shui is all about bringing the Five Elements into your space to balance and raise your vibe, but there's nothing more powerful than actually being in the Elements. Here are five rituals you can do to connect with the Five Elements and sync you with the season or to change your mood.

Forest Bathing: Wood

People have been worshiping and connecting with trees on a spiritual level since ancient times. And scientific studies now confirm that being in the presence of trees helps with mental health issues including anxiety, attention deficit hyperactivity disorder (ADHD), and depression; helps with headaches; and improves concentration. Forest bathing is a Japanese tradition that means "taking in the forest," and it's about experiencing the forest in the most basic way with your five senses. Here's how to do it: Take a walk in a forest (or wooded area), clear your mind, and open your senses. Don't think, but take in everything you see with your eyes; feel the leaves with your hands; touch a tree and feel the bark; splash your fingers in a creek; smell the fresh scent of leaves or flowers; find some mint or a blackberry and taste it; and listen to the birds, the trees swaying in the wind, or the hiss of the cicadas. Spend as much time as often as you can in the forest. This ritual channels major wood element vibes and is one you can do to feel inspired.

Sunbathing: Fire

The sun is the most important source of life for us earthlings! The first sunbathers were ancient Greeks, Egyptians, Romans, and Persians who soaked in their gardens. Sunlight kills bacteria, provides us with vitamin D, and is said to help lower blood pressure, increase serotonin, and increase testosterone levels. It's also known to help combat insomnia — no wonder you get such a good night's sleep after a day at the beach. Sunbathing is a natural and intuitive form of therapy; simply go outside for 20 minutes and soak in the rays. Hydrate well and don't overdo it. Early morning or near sunset are also good times for some sun therapy, when you can actually look at the sun. This ritual channels major fire element vibes and is one you can do to help you manifest your goals.

Earthing: Earth

Studies show that walking barefoot on the earth can help diminish chronic pain and fatigue, promote deep sleep, increase your energy, help with PMS, help with jet lag, and protect you from harmful EMFs. It also helps with the development of the nervous system and brain development (my three-year-old son actually doesn't wear hard-sole shoes yet for this reason). Electrons are released into your body that can neutralize free radicals when you walk barefoot on the earth. To feel the benefits of earthing, simply walk barefoot on the grass, dirt, rocks, or sand for 30 minutes a day. This ritual channels major earth element vibes and is one you can do when you need grounding or the healing energy of the earth.

Stargazing: Metal

Stargazing is an ancient tradition that reminds us how expansive and abundant our universe is. It can inspire you to find your inner potential, and it can be a good reminder of the ebb and flow of life to watch the cyclical movement of the stars. To stargaze (and, bonus, moon-bathe), find the light of the moon coming through your window and soak it in for 20 minutes. Notice what phase the moon is in; then look at the constellations and stars around the moon. Using the moon as a reference point helps you track the flow of the stars on a seasonal basis. If you're feeling super fun and spiritual, take your clothes off and lie down under the stars as naked as you want and soak in the energy. Keep an open mind and heart, and let the energy fill you up. This ritual channels major metal vibes and is one you can do when you need to feel focused and calm.

Soaking: Water

People have always used water as a calming therapy to restore and to experience transformation. Think of the Roman baths or the water rituals used in so many different religious ceremonies. Soaking in water restores circulation, increases mental clarity, reduces inflammation, eases stress, helps with insomnia, and in some cases helps rid your body of toxins. To feel the benefits, soak in a bathtub for 20 minutes. Add Epsom salts, a drop of your favorite essential oil, or rose petals, and surround the tub with candles. As you soak, feel how each part of your body, from the tips of your toes to the top of your head, experiences water. Clear your mind and notice the temperature, how the water lifts your body up, and the sound it makes. After soaking, dry off and rub coconut or jojoba oil into your skin. This ritual channels major water vibes and is one you can do when you need clarity or redirection in your life.

Citrus Blessing

I love this Citrus Blessing because it's all about adding a burst of happiness to your life and can double as a wealth ritual. It's transcendental and works on a spiritual level, meaning it will shift your energy by aligning your mind, body, and spirit, signaling to the universe that you're ready for a major dose of joy (or wealth).

SUPPLIES: 9 oranges, 1 large bowl

Ground Yourself

Center yourself with a meditation and repeat your favorite grounding mantra or prayer nine times.

Prepare the Bowl

Fill your bowl three-quarters of the way with water. Tear each orange rind into 9 pieces for a total of 81 peels. Tear the peels into small pieces and place them into the water.

Perform the Ritual

Start at your front door. Hold the bowl with one hand and make the expelling mudra with the other: forefinger and pinky pointed out, thumb holding middle and ring fingers. Dip your mudra fingers in the water and flick it into your space. Work your way around your space clockwise and flick water everywhere: on furniture, in closets, in bathrooms, in the garage. Let your intuition guide you.

It's key to visualize all the negative energy dispelling from your space when you flick the citrus water. Imagine the negativity melting away like in *The Wizard of Oz* when the Wicked Witch disintegrates as she's hit with water. Repeat your favorite mantra as you work through your space.

Seal the Ritual and Have Faith

At the end of the ritual, stand still and do your Personal Activation Ritual visualizing that your space is filled with new uplifting energy.

walk the nine-star path

This is a powerful sage ceremony that can dramatically shift the energy inside your home. Use this amped-up sage ritual when you want to achieve major transformation and results. It's for when you need to shake up the energy in your home, when you are working to manifest big goals, or if something negative has happened in your home and you want to clear the lingering low vibes. You can do it as often as you like. I perform this ritual for all of my clients, and I do it in my home about once a month (while I sage almost daily).

SUPPLIES: sage wand, abalone shell, feather, Energy Map of your home, Nine-Star Path illustration

Align the Nine-Star Path to Your Home Energy Map
Look at the illustration with numbers in each square of the Energy Map and arrows (page 165): that's the path of the Nine Stars. Mark the numbers on the Energy Map of your own space. You are going to use this map to move through the layout of your home according to the numbers, starting with 1 and ending at 9.

Know Your Intentions
Get clear on your intentions and why you are doing the ritual before you start. Perhaps this means getting crystal clear on the major goals you're working on manifesting; or maybe you want to clear the negative energy from an argument and your focus is to call in peace and love. Whatever it is, know what you want before walking the Nine-Star Path.

Sage

Now walk the Nine-Star Path through your home. You can do your entire downstairs floor, or you can focus on walking the path in one room. Take your time so you walk in the right order. Start at number one, think about your intentions, sage the area by blowing the smoke in all corners, and repeat the Six True Syllables as you do it: *Om Mani Padme Hum* (see page 33). Do this until you end up in the ninth area. When you reach the ninth area, send your intentions into the universe and into infinity. Declare, "And it is done."

Have Faith

Know that your space is immediately energetically different and have faith that what you want to manifest is on its way to you. Look for signs that you're receiving what you want.

Variations

If you don't like using sage, you can use palo santo, or you can use sound like a bell, gong, or clapping your hands. If you can't walk through your home or if you can't physically be in your home, you can trace the Nine-Star Path with your finger on your Energy Map, visualizing every area of your space and repeating the mantra in every area just as if you were walking it physically.

breakthrough ritual

The Breakthrough Ritual has been performed since ancient times and is one I use frequently. When you enact this ritual, you're tapping into the vibration of all of those who've done it in the past, and those performing it presently, and the profound changes they've experienced with it. I turned to this ritual when I had a newborn and work had dried up for both me and my husband. My teachers had told me about the power of the Breakthrough Ritual, and I felt called to do it. Less than one month later, my husband landed a huge job.

The Breakthrough Ritual is a powerful energy adjustment you perform on the exterior of your home to dramatically shift the energy both inside and outside your home. The Breakthrough Ritual is meant to be performed if something traumatic happened in your house, either before or while you're there; for example, if someone died in the house or if a terrible argument occurred. It can also be used if you need major help in life and you've tried everything else; if you bought your home because the previous owner went into fore-closure (you want to shift that energy); if you're facing divorce or financial bankruptcy; or if you're experiencing a major health issue. It's also perfect for when you want to take your life to the next level.

The Breakthrough Ritual works on a transcendental level, mean-ing you're removing low-vibe spirits from your property and inviting high-vibe spirits in. You're also fixing energetic blocks inside and outside your home. If you don't believe in spirits, that's totally fine. You can then focus on the fact that you're dramatically changing the energetics of your home.

Typically, the Breakthrough Ritual is performed by a Feng Shui pro-fessional, but you have the power to do it yourself. Before you start, get clear on your intentions. Know why you are doing this ritual. What do you want to get out of it? Focus on one to three things you want to manifest. Know the outcome you want before you perform the ritual; the universe can't bring it to you unless you know it and declare it.

Gather Ingredients

There are several ingredients you'll need for this ritual:

+ **2 POUNDS DRY UNCOOKED RICE.** You might need to use more or less depending on the size of your property. Your bowl should be empty at the end of the ritual.

+ **100-PROOF VODKA.** Vodka activates the mixture. Use an unopened bottle (any size will work) for your ceremony.

+ **A LARGE BOWL.** The bowl can be made of metal, ceramic, or any other nonporous material.

+ **108 MALA BEAD STRING.** Mala beads are used for prayer; you can get them online or at a metaphysical, crystal, or yoga shop. You will use the beads to repeat a mantra 108 times.

+ **1 TEASPOON CINNABAR POWDER.** Cinnabar is a traditional powder used since ancient times for this ceremony. It comes from volcanic or hot spring activity from the very center of the earth and is considered a powerful mineral to activate rituals. It represents heart (because it comes from the heart of the earth) and fire. The fire element in Feng Shui symbolizes the realization of your goals. Cinnabar clears your space of negative spirits and adds blessing to your home.

A NOTE ON CINNABAR

Cinnabar contains traces of mercury and in large quantities is considered toxic. However, I've been taught that the small amounts you'll use for this ritual are not harmful to you or to any wildlife that may come in contact with it. Cinnabar is sold online in very small quantities, teaspoon-size pouches, and you do not need more than this amount for the ritual. That said, please wash your hands and bowl thoroughly afterward just to be cautious. If you don't want to use cinnabar, you can use 1 teaspoon of chili powder or paprika as a substitution as long as your intentions are in place.

If you decide to swap out an ingredient or make another adjustment to the traditional method laid out here, that's fine — just be sure your intentions are in place. For example: I'm using vodka that's already been opened, but I'm anointing it for this ceremony and it will work as it's intended to.

Activate the Ritual

Before performing the Breakthrough Ritual, you'll want to ground yourself and activate the ritual you're about to do. Remember your Personal Activation Ritual (see Step 2).

Repeat your mantra nine times. The traditional mantra used for the Breakthrough Ritual is the Sanskrit heart-calming mantra: *Gate Gate Paragate Parasamgate Bodhi Svaha.*

Use your mudra. The traditional mudra used for the Breakthrough Ritual is the Dhyana mudra, or open heart mudra (see page 31). If this mudra doesn't resonate with you, you can use prayer hands or any mudra that you would use in your Personal Activation Ritual.

Pulling it all together: Hold the mudra of your choice, focus your eyes on something peaceful (I like to look at the sky), and repeat your mantra nine times. Ground yourself, calm your energy, and ask the universe (or whatever spirit you speak to) to energize the ritual you're about to perform.

You have now activated your Breakthrough Ritual.

Perform the Ritual

Fill the bowl with rice.

Add the cinnabar powder to the rice.

Use the cap of the vodka to measure out nine capfuls of vodka and pour each into the bowl of rice.

Use the middle finger of your right hand to mix the ingredients together in the bowl while reciting the Six True Syllables mantra, *Om Mani Padme Hum,* 108 times. Use your mala bead necklace to keep track of repeating the mantra.

After you've mixed the ingredients and said the mantra 108 times, the mixture is ready.

Go outside and start at the entrance to your house. Toss three handfuls of the rice mixture straight up into the air as high as possible using the uplifting mudra (palms open), reciting *Om Mani Padme Hum* with each throw. Visualize that you are raising the energy of your home into infinity, sending a message out into the universe that you are ready to transform your life. You're elevating your energy to a new level.

Toss three handfuls of rice parallel to the ground, aiming toward the exterior of the lot and repeating *Om Mani Padme Hum* with each throw. Visualize that your problems are disappearing and that all of your negativity is leaving your property.

Toss three handfuls straight down to the ground while repeating *Om Mani Padme Hum* with each toss. Visualize that you're planting all your desires into the ground so that they will grow.

Work your way around the property in a clockwise or counterclockwise direction, whichever feels right to you. Throw the rice up in the air, parallel, or down on the ground according to your intuition. With each throw continue to recite the Six True Syllables and visualize what you want to achieve with the ritual.

When you return to the Mouth of Chi, toss three more handfuls of rice into the sky, reciting the Six True Syllables. Your bowl should be empty at the end of the ritual. Take a moment and visualize the outcomes that you expect to happen. Repeat your mantra nine times along with your mudra of choice, and imagine everything you desire is coming to you rapidly. Then say to yourself, "And it is done."

Complete the Ritual

Have complete faith that your desires are coming to you. Know that you have dramatically changed the energy of your home by pouring your energy into this ritual using your body (through mudras), your words (through mantras), and your mind (your intentions). This has an immediate effect on your surroundings because everything around you holds energy and has absorbed all the energy you just emitted. Take a moment and see how your surroundings feel — perhaps lighter?

Know that you have just performed the most powerful Feng Shui ritual and energy adjustment that has been used for centuries. Don't worry about being perfect. Even if you missed something small, as long as your intentions are in place, the ritual will work. Leave the rice on the property indefinitely or for at least 24 hours. This is now your practice; feel free to use it whenever you're called to do so. Look for clues that your desires are materializing in your life and celebrate them. You have to acknowledge them in order to receive more.

spiritual practices to elevate your energy

Over the years, I've tried just about every holistic practice I could find. Some of those practices fell away, and there are others that I turn to time and time again for their positive benefits.

Acupuncture

Like Feng Shui, acupuncture is an arm of Traditional Chinese Medicine that uses the Five Elements to move energy around the body by inserting thin needles into various points on the skin. Acupuncture helps to increase energy flow in the body. It is recognized to help with chronic pain, menstrual cramps, infertility, and various other ailments. I used acupuncture when I was struggling to balance my hormones and get pregnant. I got pregnant a few weeks after my first session, and I believe acupuncture radically shifted the energy in my body to help me conceive. In my experience, the needles didn't hurt going in, though there was some tingling around certain insertion points. Otherwise, it was a pleasant experience. I'm a big believer in seeking out holistic health resources, and I recommend using acupuncture as a complement, not a replacement, to seeing a medical doctor. Decide what's best for you.

Tapping

Tapping helps change your energy through your emotions and helps rewire the subconscious brain. I love this practice because it's something you can do on your own. It works like acupuncture in that you tap on different points of your body to change and restore energy flow. Instead of using needles, you use your fingers to tap on various pressure points of your body. Many tapping experts offer free online videos, or you can find a local practitioner. (We used it so often in my house that my husband became a certified practitioner.)

Massage

If I were a queen, I would have a masseuse to follow me around 24-7 to give me massages on demand! Besides the obvious benefit of feeling amazing, massage helps increase circulation and eliminate toxins in the body. It gets the energy flowing, reduces anxiety, helps you sleep better, and has many more benefits. Massage is a common treatment in TCM specifically because it reaches deep into the body and (like acupuncture) accesses meridian points that clear blocks so that energy can flow with ease.

Dry Brushing

Dry brushing is an Ayurvedic practice that exfoliates your skin, helps with circulation, and promotes your body's natural lymphatic cleansing process. It also feels really good — my skin always tingles with energy after I dry-brush. Most health food stores sell dry brushes — they typically have a long wooden handle and a loofa-like brush at the end with soft bristles. I usually dry-brush my skin just before I shower. Start with the bottoms of your feet, brushing in a circular motion, and work your way to your heart, then to the top of your head. I brush a little more vigorously where I have more fat and muscle, and go more gentle on tender areas. Don't forget the lymphatic areas of your armpits, elbows, and behind your knees. Shower, then rub your body with an oil like coconut oil. Do it once a week for best results.

Cold-Water Showers

I used to spend weekends at the Turkish bathhouses in New York City, where I sat in saunas, floated in pools, and — when I felt brave enough — hopped into cold-water pools. It was totally shocking and yet so refreshing; I always left feeling like a new person. Now I take freezing-cold showers because it's totally invigorating. A cold-water shower gets your blood pumping to your organs, which helps your overall circulation and health. Cold water is less drying than hot water for your skin, which can make your skin look better. Cold-water showers have also been known to relieve feelings of stress and depression by stimulating electrical impulses of the nerve endings that go to the brain. If you can't handle taking cold-water showers, try at least blasting yourself with cold water for a few minutes before you get out.

Sound Baths

If you haven't experienced a sound bath, I highly recommend finding and going to a local event. They're often offered at yoga studios. Sound has been used for thousands of years for its therapeutic effects. It helps with relaxation, stress, insomnia, and pain management. I gravitate toward sound when I'm experiencing physical pain — and many of us, of course, turn to music to heal on a spiritual level. When you attend a sound bath, you'll usually lie down on your back (bring a yoga mat and pillow) and the artist will play sound bowls and gongs of different notes and frequencies to restore your mind and body, sending you into a meditative state. Different classes have different goals of channeling energy, so check to see which one *resonates* (ha) with you (though I don't think you can go wrong).

Aura Cleanse

Your aura is the electromagnetic energy field that surrounds you. It contains different layers that affect your overall health, feelings, thoughts, and behaviors. It's basically what you're putting out into the universe, also known as your vibe. And it also shapes the way you experience the world because everything is filtered through your aura. When you get stuck in a feeling, thought pattern, or behavior pattern you don't like, you can cleanse your aura to reset your vibe. Here's how: Stand under flowing water — whether that's a shower, a waterfall, or a good rainfall. Feel the water hitting the top of your head and flowing down to your feet while imagining all of the low-vibe energy that's been sticking to you washing away. Imagine all of the negative emotions, behaviors, and mental clutter washing away from your body. Afterward, you can wear a protective crystal, like black tourmaline, to filter out the negative and keep your aura clean.

Negativity Cleanse

Surrounding yourself with negativity creates major low-vibe energy that can stick to the walls in your home, your furniture, your plants, and definitely to you. It drags you down to a place where opportunities don't flow into your life, you feel unwell, and you attract low-vibe people in your life. On the other hand, positivity raises your vibe and the energy levels of your home to a place where opportunities come to you more easily and with less effort. Positive words, including mantras, have even been known to benefit the health of sick people and animals. If you're attracting a lot of low energy into your life, this cleanse is my favorite way to get back on track.

STOP GOSSIPING

Gossiping is always negative. Do you ever gossip with a friend only to feel yucky afterward? And then you have to worry if it's going to get back to the person you were talking about? Stop talking about other people. When you shift the focus to yourself, your dreams, your goals, and your friend's dreams and goals, you're creating a positive conversation that enhances your vibration.

STOP COMPLAINING

Complaining is super low energy because you're not practicing gratitude, which is the highest vibrational state — next to love — that you can be in. By complaining, you're pointing out the lack in your life and sending a message to the universe that you're unable to receive what you want. Next time you feel the urge to complain, focus instead on being grateful for something you have.

STOP COMPARING YOURSELF TO OTHERS

This is especially difficult when you're on social media, but we need to stop scrolling through and comparing our lives to someone else's. Stop scrutinizing people's careers, bodies, and families. Emotions are the best way to check your vibration levels. If what you see on other people's social media feeds makes you sad (or happy with Schadenfreude), you aren't operating at a high-vibe level. Limit your time on social media for 30 days and unfollow people whom you compare yourself to.

LIMIT YOUR NEWS INTAKE

I'm not suggesting being totally in the dark about what's happening in the world, but with 24-7 news feeds on television and the Internet, it can be a negativity overload. In excess, the news can create fear, anxiety, stress, and sadness in your life where you might not otherwise have had any. Limit yourself to the headlines midday to stay informed; do not check the news before bed or right when you wake up, when your subconscious is most impressionable.

thank you!

First and foremost, I want to thank my husband, Thomas Cantley, for his endless support, inspiration, and love. Without him, this book wouldn't have been written. Thank you to my parents for their love and support and to Rebecca Gaborek for her invaluable friendship. Thank you to all of my teachers (many of whom I've never met), who inspire me through your books and podcasts. Thank you to my agent, Pamela Harty. And lastly, this book would not be possible without Storey Publishing and especially Liz Bevilacqua, who championed it every step of the way.

177

resources

The International Feng Shui Guild: www.ifsguild.org

My favorite crystal resource: www.energymuse.com

My favorite book on the Five Elements: *Creating Luminous Spaces*
by Maureen K. Calamia

Energy Map

WEALTH	FAME	LOVE
FAMILY	WELLNESS	CHILDREN & CREATIVITY
KNOWLEDGE & SPIRITUALITY	CAREER & LIFE JOURNEY	RELATIONSHIPS & TRAVEL

front door

index

Page numbers in *italic* indicate figures; page numbers in **bold** indicate tables.

179

stoves, 132
subconscious, 9, 20
sunbathing, 160
superstitions, misconceptions about, 11
Swarovski crystal, 81–82

T
tablets, 153
Tai Chi, 64
tapping, 172–173
Taurus, 64
TCM. *See* Traditional Chinese Medicine
Third Eye, 40
Tibetan singing bowls, 50
tradition, incorporating, 12
Traditional Chinese Medicine (TCM)
    Feng Shui as arm of, 12
    Five Elements and, 53, 64
travel
    balancing and enhancing, 107–109

Energy Map and, 56
scents for, 85

U
Universal Laws, 8–9
Universal Mind, 38

V
vegetables, 154
Vibration, Law of
    mantras and, 32–33
    overview of, 8–9
    Personal Activation Rituals and, 26, 28
vintage furniture, 135
vision boards, 35
visualization, activation rituals and, 28–29
vodka, 168

W
Walk the Nine-Star Path, 164–166, *165*
water, 72, 73
water crystals, mantras and, 32
water element, **66–67**, 162

wealth
    balancing and enhancing, 116–117
    crystals for, 80
    Energy Map and, 56
    scents for, 85
wellness
    Energy Map and, 58
    limiting beliefs and, 21–22
    scents for, 85
wellness, balancing and enhancing, 124–125
white color, 84
wind chimes, 82–83
windows, 94–95
wood element, **66–67**, 160

Y
yellow color, 83
yin and yang, 65, 66–67
Yoga poses, inner voice and, 40–41

183

184